OLD WEST SURREY

SOME NOTES AND MEMORIES

BY

GERTRUDE JEKYLL

With 330 Illustrations from Photographs by the Author

Copyright © 2018 Read Books Ltd.
This book is copyright and may not be
reproduced or copied in any way without
the express permission of the publisher in writing

British Library Cataloguing-in-Publication Data
A catalogue record for this book is available from
the British Library

Homesteading

Broadly defined, homesteading is a lifestyle of self-sufficiency. It is characterized by subsistence agriculture, home preservation of foodstuffs, and it may or may not also involve the small scale production of textiles, clothing, and craftwork for household use or sale. Pursued in different ways around the world — and in different historical eras — homesteading is generally differentiated from rural village or commune living by isolation (either socially or physically) of the homestead. This is not the case any longer however, with 'homesteading' principles witnessing a massive resurgence in urban areas as well as in the countryside. Use of the term in the United States dates back to the Homestead Act (1862) and before, whereas in the UK the term 'small holder' is the rough equivalent.

The attractiveness of back-to-the-land movements dates from the Roman era, and has been noted in Asian poetry and philosophy tracts as well. The ideas of modern homesteading proponents, such as Ralph Borsodi (an American agrarian theorist and practical experimenter, interested in methods of self-reliant living, especially so during the Great Depression), rapidly gained in popularity. Yet Self-sufficiency movements in the 1990s and 2000s began to apply the concept to urban and suburban settings, known as urban homesteading. This latter concept incorporates small-scale, sustainable agriculture and homemaking; often more difficult due to space restrictions, though incredibly rewarding! With worsening economic conditions and increased interest in organic and sustainable living, many people are turning to vegetable gardening as a supplement to their family's diet. Food grown in the back yard consumes little if any fuel for shipping or maintenance, and the grower can be sure of what exactly was used to grow it. Such forms of organic gardening have become increasingly popular for the modern home gardener.

Whether you have a massive plot, or just a few planters, growing vegetables is satisfying as well as healthy. It also has a long history, dating back to French Renaissance 'potagers' and Victorian Kitchen gardens. Kitchen gardens in turn have emerged from the 'Cottage Garden', the earliest of which were much more practical than their modem descendants. These were working class gardens, with an emphasis on vegetables and herbs, along with some fruit trees, perhaps a beehive and even livestock, with flowers only used to fill any spaces in-between. Through each person using the land and resources available to them, 'homesteading' has quickly become part of the 'permaculture' movement; a branch of ecological design and engineering, that develops sustainable architecture and self-maintained agricultural systems modelled from natural ecosystems. The term originally referred to 'permanent agriculture' but was expanded to stand also for 'permanent culture', as it was seen that social aspects were integral to a truly sustainable system (as inspired by Masanobu Fukuoka's 'natural farming' philosophy).

As stated by Bill Mollison, 'Permaculture is a philosophy of working with, rather than against nature; of protracted and thoughtful observation rather than protracted and thoughtless labour; and of looking at plants and animals in all their functions, rather than treating any area as a single product system.' Its core tenets revolve around care for the earth, care for the people and return of surplus; a key element is maximising useful connections between the various components, and synergy of the final design. This may sound hard to achieve, but those working with a 'homesteading' ethos are performing many of these roles already! By making or reusing one's own foodstuffs, textiles (repairing and sewing), crafts, household objects / whatsoever else, this helps to minimise waste, human labour and energy input. We hope the current reader is inspired by this book to try some sustainable homesteading of their own. Enjoy!

OLD WEST SURREY

PREFACE

So many and so great have been the changes within the last half-century, that I have thought it desirable to note, while it may yet be done, what I can remember of the ways and lives and habitations of the older people of the working class of the country I have lived in almost continuously ever since I was a very young child.

It is the south-western corner of the county of Surrey; so near indeed to the actual corner, that the adjoining portions of Hampshire and Sussex come within a radius of a very few miles, and are considered as within the district. After all, geographical distinctions are purely arbitrary, and only really appreciable on the map, where they show in different colours; whereas, in the real world, one steps without knowing it from Surrey into Hampshire on the dry heath-land, and out of Surrey into Sussex from one clay puddle into the next, without being aware in either case that the land is called by another name.

The practical boundaries of our country that we commonly call West Surrey, without any reference to parliamentary or other authorised divisions, are the long chalk line of the Hog's Back on the north, with its eastern prolongation beyond Guildford, and the Weald of Sussex to the south.

We hardly ever go northward beyond the Hog's Back, except of course in the train, which does not count, and we do not go much down to the Weald. We like to look out from our southward-facing hills and see right across the Weald to the long, dim, blue-hazy line of the South Downs, and to know that beyond this is the sea, and then France, and the rest of the world.

But we wander a long way east and west in the pleasant country of the sandy hills, from the still wild lands south of Dorking on the east, right away to Woolmer Forest and Gilbert White's country in the west.

When I was a child all this tract of country was undiscovered; now, alas! it is overrun.

It is impossible to grudge others the enjoyment of its delights, and yet one cannot but regret, that the fact of its being now thickly populated and much built over, has necessarily robbed it of its older charms of peace and retirement.

Formerly, within a mile or two of one's home, it was a rare thing to see a stranger, and people's lives went leisurely. Now, the strain and throng and unceasing restlessness that have been induced by all kinds of competition, and by ease of communication, have invaded this quiet corner of the land. In the older days, London might have been at a distance of two hundred miles. Now one never can forget that it is at little more than an hour's journey.

Common things of daily use, articles of furniture and ordinary household gear, that I remember in every cottage and farmhouse, have passed into the dealers' hands, and are now sold as curiosities and antiquities. Cottages, whose furniture and appointments had come through several generations, are now furnished with cheap pretentious articles, got up with veneer and varnish and shoddy material. The floor is covered with oilcloth, the walls have a paper of shocking design, and are hung with cheap oleographs and tradesmen's illustrated almanacs.

This is the modern exchange for the solid furniture of pure material and excellent design, and for the other things of daily use—all the best possible for their varied purposes—that will presently be shown and described.

It must be understood that these notes and memories make no claim to a thorough or comprehensive description of people or objects; the most that they can attempt is to give some idea of the general aspects of the older country life and gear, and possibly to convey to the sympathetic reader some slight impression of their character. They are for the main part the recollections of one individual, refreshed and augmented by recent conversations with a few friends in the immediate neighbourhood.

Among those who have helped me in this way, I should like to make special acknowledgment to Colonel and Mrs. Godwin-Austen of Shalford House; Miss Ewart of Coneyhurst; Miss Kiddell, formerly schoolmistress at Bramley; Mr. James Jackson, engineer and builder, of Bramley; Mr. George Tickner, carpenter and builder, of Milford; John Eastwood, Esq. of Enton; the Rev. Gerald S. Davies, of the Charterhouse; Mr. Russell G. Davey, of Guildford; the Rev. W. H. Winn, Rector of Dunsfold, and the Rev. George Chilton.

Since the desirability of this, however fragmentary, record of the ways and things of the older days occurred to me, I have regretted that I did not think of it thirty years ago. But it is only now, when one becomes aware how little of the old is yet remaining, that the degree of the change is more clearly to be observed.

PREFACE

But when it became evident that the old articles of cottage furniture and equipment were being dispersed, I lost no opportunity, chiefly at country sales, of securing things that might be considered typical. These articles, with others of a like nature lent by friends, form the subjects of the greater number of the illustrations.

G. J.

CONTENTS

CHAPTER I
COTTAGES AND FARMS 1–43

CHAPTER II
THE OLD FURNITURE OF COTTAGE AND FARMHOUSE 44–78

CHAPTER III
THE COTTAGE FIRESIDE 79–100

CHAPTER IV
CANDLE-LIGHT AND CANDLESTICKS 101–115

CHAPTER V
COTTAGE ORNAMENTS 116–140

CHAPTER VI
CROCKERY AND TABLE WARE 141–156

CHAPTER VII
HOME INDUSTRIES 157–168

CHAPTER VIII
VARIOUS ARTICLES FOUND IN COTTAGES . . . 169–180

CHAPTER IX
TOOLS AND RURAL INDUSTRIES 181–210

CONTENTS

CHAPTER X
THE CARTER'S PRIDE 211-217

CHAPTER XI
OLD COUNTRY FOLK—THEIR WAYS OF SPEECH . . 218-228

CHAPTER XII
OLD COUNTRY FOLK—SOME OF THEIR WAYS . . 229-248

CHAPTER XIII
OLD COUNTRY FOLK—THEIR CLOTHING 249-267

CHAPTER XIV
COTTAGE GARDENS 268-277

CHAPTER XV
FOUND IN THE WOODS 278-281

CHAPTER XVI
GODALMING 282-295

CHAPTER XVII
CHURCHYARDS THEN AND NOW 296-302

CHAPTER XVIII
THE SMUGGLERS 303-316

LIST OF ILLUSTRATIONS

	PAGE
OLD WEST SURREY	*Frontispiece*
HALF-TIMBERED COTTAGE, NOW ALTERED, HAMBLEDON	2
WEATHER-TILED COTTAGES, KIRKFORD	2
TIMBER-FRAMED COTTAGES, ELSTEAD	3
TILE-HUNG COTTAGES, MILFORD	3
TILE-HUNG COTTAGE, TILTHAM'S GREEN . . .	4
AN OLD COTTAGE, ELSTEAD	6
BOWBRICK'S COTTAGE	7
BOWBRICK	8
STONE PAVING AT COTTAGE ENTRANCE	8
PAVED COTTAGE ENTRANCE	9
THE BRICK OVEN—OUTSIDE	10
STONE-PAVED COTTAGE ENTRANCE	11
A PAVING OF RIPPLE-MARKED STONE	12
IRON-STONE PITCHING WITH BARGATE KERB . . .	13
THE WELL-WINCH	14
DAIRY COURT, UNSTEAD FARM	15
UNSTEAD FARM	17
THE DAIRY YARD, UNSTEAD FARM	18
THE GREAT FARM KITCHEN	20
THE DAIRY	21
LEAD VENTILATOR	22
THE IRON ROOM	23
INSIDE THE BARN	24
THE RICK-SETTLE	25
OAK POST AND RAIL FENCE	26
FROM THE RICKYARD	27
THE FIVE-BARRED GATE	28
AN OAK STILE	29
THE SEWAGE PUMP	30
FARMHOUSE AT SHERE, WITH WALLS ROUGH-CAST .	31
HURST FARM, MILFORD	32
THE BACK OF THE FARMHOUSE	32
BACK OF THE FARMHOUSE	33
A DOG-GATE	34
IRON DROP-HANDLE	34

LIST OF ILLUSTRATIONS

	PAGE
BACK OF WYATT'S ALMSHOUSES	35
GRANARY AND WAGGON-SHED	36
THE MILLER	37
THE MILL-HOUSE, ENTON	38
STEPS NEAR THE OLD MILL	39
BACK STEPS, ENTON MILL	40
HALF-TIMBERED COTTAGES, EASHING	41
NEW COTTAGES OF AN OLD PATTERN	41
A NEW COTTAGE	42
WALL WITH GARNETED JOINTS	43
OAK TABLE, SEVEN FEET LONG	45
OAK FORM	46
WOODEN TRENCHERS, FLOUR-BARREL, AND SCOOP	47
LINEN HUTCH AND EIGHT-LEGGED TABLE	48
ROUND OAK TABLE	49
THREE-LEGGED OAK TABLE	49
JOINT STOOL	50
JOINT STOOL WITH TABLE-TOP	50
CARVED OAK LINEN-HUTCH	51
OAK DRESSER WITH WILLOW WARE	52
ELM THREE-LEGGED TABLE	53
OAK CLOTHES HUTCH	54
OAK DESK	54
OAK BIBLE-BOX	55
STANDING DESK	55
WHEEL-BACK WINDSOR CHAIR	56
OLD RAIL-BACK AND ORDINARY MODERN WINDSOR CHAIRS	57
WHEEL-BACK WINDSOR ARMCHAIR	58
RUSH-BOTTOMED CHAIR	59
TWO RUSH-BOTTOMED OAK ARMCHAIRS	60
BLACK-STAINED RUSH-BOTTOMED ARMCHAIR	61
WICKER-SEATED ANGLE CHAIR	62
A GOOD EIGHT-DAY CLOCK	63
COTTAGE 24-HOUR CLOCK	64
DUTCH CLOCK	65
OAK CHEST OF DRAWERS	66
EARLY BRASS KEYHOLE SCUTCHEONS	66
HANDLE AND KEYHOLE SCUTCHEONS	66
OAK CRADLE, SEVENTEENTH CENTURY	67
BABY-RUNNER	68
SALT-BOX	69
KNIFE-BOX	69
KNIFE-TRAY AND PEWTER TANKARD	69
COFFEE-MILL	70
'CAT'	70

LIST OF ILLUSTRATIONS

	PAGE
LARGE MOUSE-TRAP, TEN INCHES LONG	71
TWO DEAD-FALL MOUSE-TRAPS	71
BED-WAGGON	72
COPPER WARMING-PAN	73
SOME VERY OLD KITCHEN IMPLEMENTS	74
BRASS LADLE AND SKIMMER	75
IRON SKEWERS	75
HEAVY IRON NUT-CRACKERS	75
SUGAR-NIPPERS	75
VERY OLD IRON SNUFFERS AND SCISSORS	76
PIPE-CLEANER, BRASS BOX-IRON AND STAND	76
WICKER BIRD-CAGE	77
THE BRICK OVEN	77
OVEN PEEL	78
POCKET LANTERN	78
CLAY PIPES	79
COTTAGE FIREPLACE AND INGLE-NOOK	80
CHIMNEY-CRANE WITH THREE MOTIONS	82
CHIMNEY-CRANE WITH WROUGHT-IRON ORNAMENT	83
TWO VERY OLD HANGERS	84
HANGERS OF ORDINARY FORM	85
LARGE IRON POT ON HANGER	86
FIRE-DOGS	87
TWO ANCIENT CAST-IRON FIRE-DOGS	87
WROUGHT-IRON CUP-DOGS	88
BASKET SPIT	89
PRONGED ROASTING SPIT	89
SPIT-RACK	90
CAST-IRON FIRE-BACK	91
FIRE-BACK OF FRENCH DESIGN	91
BRONZE SKILLETS	92
BRASS SKILLETS ON TRIVETS, SMALL IRON POT, AND CHEESE CAULDRON	92
LONG-HANDLED COPPER FRYING-PAN	93
IRON TRIVETS	93
STANDING TOASTING-FORKS	94
TOASTER AND POTATO-RAKER	95
BAKING IRON	95
FIRE-IRONS AND VERY OLD BELLOWS	96
BRAND-TONGS	97
BELLOWS	98
WHEEL AND FAN BELLOWS	99
IDLE-BACK	100
PEELED RUSHES FOR RUSH-LIGHTS	102
GREASE-PANS	103

LIST OF ILLUSTRATIONS

	PAGE
Rush-Lights after being Dipped in Grease	103
Six Rush-Light Holders	104
Rush-Light Holders. The Tallest 9½ Inches	104
Rush-Light in the Holder	105
Standing Rush-Light and Candle-Holders	106
Wooden Standing Rush-Light Holders	107
Iron Tinder-Boxes	108
Sulphur Matches	108
Brass Tinder-Box and Brass Candlestick	109
Candle-Box	109
Hanging Iron Candlestick	110
Iron Candlestick driven into Post	110
Iron Spiral Candlesticks	111
Iron Trivet and Kitchen Candlesticks	111
Iron Candlestick with Jointed Arm	112
Brass Candlesticks	113
Red Brass Candlesticks	114
Brass Candlesticks	114
Brass Snuffers and Trays	114
Flint-Lock for Igniting Tinder	115
Chimney-Piece Looking-Glass	116
Toby-Jug	117
Cow-Jug	118
Cottage Chimney Ornaments	119
Pair of Chimney Ornaments	120
A Set of Chimney Ornaments	120
Shepherd and Shepherdess	121
Sampler, Dated 1834	122
Portrait of the Worker	123
Sampler—Map of England, 1835	124
Sampler—Map of Europe, Dated 1783	124
Sampler	125
Patchwork Quilt—Eighteenth Century	126
Patchwork Quilt—Early Nineteenth Century	127
Part of a Quilt—Patchwork of Chintz	128
Part of a Patchwork Quilt—Early Nineteenth Century	129
Kettle-Holder	131
Picture in Application and Embroidery	132
The Return out of Egypt	133
Bible Pictures	134
Love and Retirement	135
The Charming Florist	135
Brass Dredgers, Pepper-Pots, Spoon, and Box	136
Pepper-Pots	137
Brass Teaspoons	138

LIST OF ILLUSTRATIONS

	PAGE
PEWTER INKSTAND	138
PEWTER INKSTANDS AND CANDLESTICK	138
TEA-CADDIES	138
PAINTED BOX	139
MARY SMITH'S MONEY-BOX	139
OAK PUZZLE MONEY-BOX	140
BONE DOMINO-BOX	140
STONE BOTTLE, NINE INCHES HIGH	142
OLD QUART MUG WITH IRON HANDLE	142
EIGHTEENTH-CENTURY STONEWARE MUGS	143
MODERN LAMBETH STONEWARE	143
LARGE STONE-WARE BOTTLES AND RED-WARE LARD-POTS	145
STONE-WARE AND EARTHENWARE PIPKINS	145
RED EARTHENWARE PITCHERS	146
DORSETSHIRE PILLS	147
GLAZED PITCHER OF NORTHERN POTTERY	148
BRISTOL WARE	149
THREE JUGS OF DIPPED WARE	149
COLOURED MUGS FROM THE NORTHERN POTTERIES	149
MUGS AND JUGS	151
SOUP TUREEN OF LANDSCAPE WARE	152
TEAPOT AND MUG OF LANDSCAPE WARE	153
VARIOUS PIECES OF LUSTRE WARE	154
BLACK WEDGWOOD WARE	154
FARM-JUG OF STAFFORDSHIRE WARE	155
THREE PATTERNS OF HAY-RAKE	156
SPINNING-WHEEL	158
THE WINDER	158
A SILK-WINDER	159
STRAW-CRUSHER	160
THE RED-WARE PAN	161
OLD SMOOTHING IRONS	162
THE IRON WASHING-LINE	162
A COTTAGER'S BEE-HIVES	163
BUTTER SCALES WITH WOODEN PANS	164
BUTTER-PRINTS	165
BUTTER SCOOP AND WOODEN SPOON	165
LARGE WOODEN SPIGOT	166
THE HEATH BROOM	167
OAK CHAIR—DATE ABOUT 1660	170
MAHOGANY CHAIR	170
TWO MAHOGANY ARMCHAIRS	170
LIGHT BEDROOM CHAIRS	171
LACQUER LOOKING-GLASS	171
LACQUER AND MAHOGANY TRAYS	173

LIST OF ILLUSTRATIONS

	PAGE
HOUR-GLASS	174
ORIENTAL AND ENGLISH PORCELAIN AND GLASS	175
PEWTER TABLE WARE	175
PEWTER MUGS	175
NEW AND OLD STONE MORTARS	176
IRON AND BRASS APOTHECARIES' MORTARS	176
PAIR OF PLATED CANDLESTICKS	177
SPECIAL CONSTABLE'S STAFF	178
SWINGING BLUDGEON	178
WOODEN RATTLE	178
LEG IRONS	179
SMALL IRON BOX, FOUR INCHES SQUARE	179
THE STOCKS, SHALFORD	180
REAPING-HOOKS AND FAG-HOOK	182
DIBBLING-IRON	185
WOODEN PLOUGH	186
FLAIL, CURB-CHAIN, AND LARGE SHEEP-BELL	187
A MOWER	188
HARVEST BOTTLES	190
ON A HARVEST BOTTLE	191
LETTERING ON A HARVEST BOTTLE	191
HORN MUGS	192
LEATHER BOTTLES—THE LARGEST 8 INCHES LONG	193
LEATHER BOTTLE, CUT TO HOLD CART-GREASE	193
THE SAW-PIT	194
THE CIDER-MILL	195
THE CIDER-PRESS	195
COPSE-CUTTER FAGGOTING UP	197
THE HURDLE-MAKER	198
SHEPHERD'S CROOK	200
MARKING-IRON AND SHEEP BELLS	200
STEEL-YARD	201
TOOL FOR CUTTING HEATH-TURF	202
CUTTING HEATH-TURF	203
THE OLD BRICKLAYER	204
TIMBER-WAGGON	205
AN OLD ROADSIDE LIMEKILN	206
THE ARCH OF MYSTERY	207
WOODEN MOLE-TRAP	210
THE CARTER'S TROPHY OF HORSE ORNAMENTS	212
SMALL BELLS AND SWINGING BRASSES	212
LATTEN BELLS	213
EAR-CAPS	214
AN OLD FARM BRIDLE	215
OLD HORSE-SHOES	215

LIST OF ILLUSTRATIONS

	PAGE
Ploughman Bringing Home the Horses	216
The Evening Drink	217
An Old Labourer	219
A Bill on a Hazel Stick	225
Model of Winnowing-Fan	231
The Cottage Porch	232
The Writer of the Autobiography	233
The Manuscript	235
Hog-Form and Cutting-Up Knife	242
Leaden Tobacco-Box	245
On the Public-House Ceiling	246
At the Red Lion	246
Old Brass Shoe-Buckles	249
Cottagers' Dress of 1850	250
The Cottage Cap	251
The Prayer-Book	252
An Old Cottage Cap	252
The Garden Wall—Outside	253
The Garden Wall—Inside	253
The Head-Handkerchief	254
The Sun-Bonnet	255
Pattens	256
The White Smock-Frock	258
The White Frock	259
An Old Sunday Smock	260
The Blacksmith	261
Some of the Old Sort in White Corduroy	263
The Plain Old Way	265
Luggage for a Journey	266
Coloured Cotton Handkerchiefs	266
'My Cluster-Rose do Blow Beautiful'	269
A Staging of Pot-Plants	269
Cluster Rose in a Cottage Garden	270
The Window Plant	271
Roses and Canterbury Bells	272
Cottagers and their Pot-Plants	273
Banksian Rose Round a Cottage Window	273
Cluster Rose on a Cottage Entrance	274
The Everlasting Pea at a Cottage Door	274
A Cottager's Border of China Asters	275
Dahlias in the Cottage Garden	276
Clipped Yews at a Cottage Entrance	277
Otter or Fox-Trap, Toasting-Fork, and Baking-Iron	278
Spring Guns	279
The Man-Trap	281

LIST OF ILLUSTRATIONS

	PAGE
The 'White Hart' Inn	283
Old Houses in the High Street	284
The 'Little George' Inn	285
The 'King's Arms'	288
Glass Bottles of a Hundred Years ago	291
Carved Cocoa-Nuts	292
Spanish Demijohn	292
Flint-Lock Blunderbuss	293
The Old Altar-Tomb	297
Grave-Boards	298
Tomb—Early Nineteenth Century—Thursley	299
Altar Tombs, 1821—Hascombe	300
A Woodland Lair	304
A Thorn Thicket	304
By Heathy Heights	305
Through Gorse-Grown Hollows	305
By the Heath Ponds	306
In a Smuggler's Lane	307
A Woodland Track	308
Old Yew on the Chalk Downs	309
The Pilgrims' Yews	310
One of the Pilgrims' Yews	311
Black Bryony	312
A Shoulder of the Downs	313
Old Track, now a Good Road	314

OLD WEST SURREY

CHAPTER I

COTTAGES AND FARMS

The changes that have taken place in rural ways of living within the last fifty years have necessitated alterations in many a humble country dwelling. Many have been swept away altogether; others have been altered in a manner that has destroyed their older character.

It is true that a good many of the older cottages were damp, or in other ways insanitary; but it is to be regretted that, where alteration or rebuilding became a necessity, it should not have been done in a way that agrees with the best traditions of the district.

No attempt is made in these pages to give anything more than a sketch of the general aspect and construction of the old cottages and farms, as an introduction to such a description of their older furniture and general equipment, and to some of the ways of their inmates, as has come within the writer's observation.

The older cottages of the district are, for the most part, built of brick-noggin—that is to say, a framing of oak filled in with brick. Sometimes the bricks were set back so as to allow of a coating of plaster. The brick surface, whether plastered or not, was usually lime-whitened, the white of the

HALF-TIMBERED COTTAGE, NOW ALTERED, HAMBLEDON

WEATHER-TILED COTTAGES, KIRDFORD

TIMBER-FRAMED COTTAGES, ELSTEAD

TILE-HUNG COTTAGES, MILFORD

lime being slightly warmed with ochre. Oftener than not the upper part was weather-tiled, or tile-hung—an excellent protection against the weather. Walking round these old cottages, there is sure to be on one side the large projection which means the wide fireplace inside, and often a separate projection of the brick oven (see p. 10).

The old roofing material was almost invariably the plain

TILE-HUNG COTTAGE, TILTHAM'S GREEN

roofing tile, though towards the Sussex border many roofs were covered with 'Horsham slabs,' of a stone that flakes into plates like thick slates.

The plain tiles were sometimes varied with others rounded at the free end like a fish-scale, or the same pattern with a small square shoulder. Often in the older examples the weather-tiles were of unusual thickness, giving an excellent effect, as in the road front of the mill building, p. 37.

COTTAGES AND FARMS

Not unfrequently plain weather-tiling was repaired with tiles of a scale or diamond pattern, or they may possibly have been originally hung together, just as they came. This happy-go-lucky way of using local material often has a good effect, as may be seen in the cottage at Kirdford and the one at Tiltham's Green. It is a matter for regret when, as is so often done now in repairing old cottage roofs or even building new ones, ridge tiles are used in place of the proper hip-tile. There is a special charm about the fine old saddle-shaped, locally-made hip-tiles, with their saw-edged profile telling well against the sky, just as there is a charm, and the satisfying conviction of a thing being exactly right, about all the building details that are of local tradition and form the local style.

Many of the older chimneys have handsome heads of a pattern whose general type is nearly always the same. They were built of thinner bricks than those of the present standard size, so that the ornament formed by the projecting courses had a certain delicacy. This shows very plainly when an old pattern of chimney is copied in the modern brick (whose height is $2\frac{1}{2}$ inches, whereas the old brick was 2 inches); the whole thing is coarsened and spoilt. Some of the older chimneys, instead of a pot on the top to help the draught or cure smoking, have an arrangement of tiles that the local bricklayer calls a 'bonnet.'

Often, in speaking of these country buildings, I have been asked what I mean or understand by the style of the country. I can only explain it thus. The local tradition in building is the crystallisation of local need, material and ingenuity. When the result is so perfect, that is to say, when the adaptation of means to ends is so satisfactory that it has held good for a long time, and that no local need or influence can change it for the better, it becomes a style, and remains fixed until other conditions arise to disturb it.

Within the last fifty years many of these disturbing influences have arisen. Ease of communication has brought slates from Wales and fir from Sweden, displacing, by their

An Old Cottage, Elstead

temptation of cheapness, the home-made tiles and honest English oak of the ancient dwellings.

The older cottages usually had two rooms on the ground floor—the living-room-kitchen, and a back kitchen, with a copper and a brick oven—and two, or sometimes three, bedrooms above. The roof was often brought down on one side to cover a lean-to, which added much to the convenience and greatly to the pictorial value of the building.

COTTAGES AND FARMS

There still exists at Bramley an old cottage of one room above and one below, the only one I now know in the country. The rooms are ten feet square; the lower one five feet nine inches to the underside of the joists. The upper room was reached by a step-ladder through an opening in the

BOWBRICK'S COTTAGE

floor. It now serves as a store to a grocery and provision business, and is a good deal obscured, from the only point from which a photograph can be taken, by a timber erection with corrugated iron roof, in which slaughtered pigs are hung till they are ready to be cut up.

But I well remember a worthy old couple named Bowbrick who lived in it. This was before the days of photographs, but here is old Bowbrick's portrait as he looked in church. He used to sit on a narrow bench at the foot of a column just opposite our pew, and his picture was done from recollection when I was about fourteen. He was nearly bald, and his head was always neatly tied up in a blue cotton handkerchief, and he wore a patch over one blind eye.

Bowbrick

There was a very old cottage in a wood about four miles from this one, since pulled down. When I knew it some additions had been made; but it was easy to see that the original structure had been a dwelling of the most primitive type; just one good-sized room, longer than square, with a thatched roof. I am glad to see that there is a picture of it in Mrs. Allingham's 'Happy England' (No. 46: 'In Wormley Wood')—a book of beautiful

Stone Paving at Cottage Entrance

pictures, that shows far better than I can attempt to describe, the charm that belongs to these old West Surrey cottages.

Paved Cottage Entrance

THE BRICK OVEN—OUTSIDE

COTTAGES AND FARMS

Many of the older cottages have a rough paving of Bargate slabs, or a pitching of the local black iron-stones, from the gate to the cottage door, or of both kinds mixed, with often a few paving-bricks. It not only looks well and is

STONE-PAVED COTTAGE ENTRANCE

durable, but as the man comes in from his work he stamps his feet as he passes over the stones, and shakes off most of the loose sandy earth that clings to his boots.

In this country of light-soiled lands, one does not see the handsome wrought-iron door-scrapers so frequent in the clay of the Weald.

These black iron-stones, that are close to the surface, have among them a large proportion with one flat edge. These are the ones that are picked out for 'pitching,' as it is called, when the stones of a pavement are laid on edge. The Bargate stone, of which there are many quarries in the Godalming district, is also used in the same way, but this is

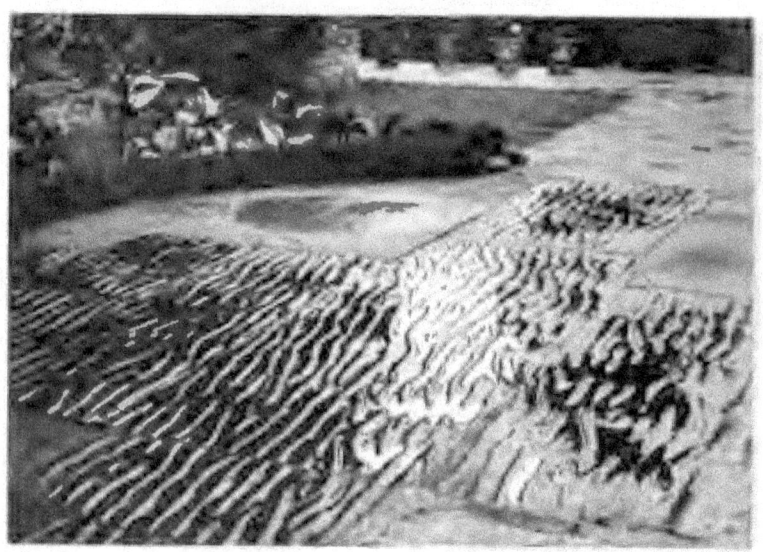

A PAVING OF RIPPLE-MARKED STONE

more expensive work, as the stones have to be trimmed to shape. During a century an iron-stone pitched pavement does not show the slightest evidence of wear.

Near, and just within the Sussex borders, may be seen here and there a pavement of large slabs of stone marked with shallow ripples, just as sea-sand is marked by the lately ebbed tide. Ages ago—millions of years—before the chalk of the downs was formed in the sea-bottom and upheaved, these ripple marks were made under shallow water. There

Iron-stone Pitching with Bargate Kerb

THE WELL-WINCH

was a quarry in the Horsham district, where they were formerly found.

Each cottage, except when they were closely grouped, had its well. Down in the valleys, where the water is near the surface, it was reached by lowering the pail by a pole with

DAIRY COURT, UNSTEAD FARM

a spring hook at the end, or, if deeper, with a winch and rope. These operations, of course, still go on, but now the pail is of clanking galvanised iron; the old wooden pail, of oak staves with iron hoops, is nearly dead.

Some of the older farmhouses are of great interest and beauty. One of the best and earliest examples in the country of the use of oak timber is Unstead Farm, a good sample of the work of rural builders of three hundred years ago. The present tiled roof was perhaps originally all Horsham slabs; a portion of the original roof remaining on the side of the paved yard, where the dairy pails and other tackle are put out, after being scalded, to dry and sweeten in the sun and air.

As in all the larger farmhouses, here was a roomy bacon-loft. Where the main kitchen chimney in these old buildings shows outside, as it generally does, and we see the wide base carried up to half or sometimes the whole height of the bedroom floor, it is an indication of a bacon-loft within. Here the bacon was hung up for smoking after being cured. Ranges of slightly-arched iron ribs stretch across the ceiling; they are studded with strong hooks for carrying the sides of bacon. The iron ribs are just far enough apart to allow the sides to hang without touching. Some lofts have six rows of them, besides rows of hooks all round the walls for hanging the smaller stuff—hams and chaps.

Nothing but wood is used in the fires for smoking bacon; oak for preference, or ash. Some use oak sawdust, but the fuel most in request is the rough outside part of oak-bark. One of the local industries is the stripping and preparation of oak-bark for tanning. In the older days oak was felled in the winter, when the sap was not in action, and winter-felled oak has the best reputation. But the bark is of so much value for tanning, that now oaks are commonly felled in May, when the sap is running and the bark will strip easily. Short forked stumps are driven into the ground to support a straight bit of branch; the pieces of stripped bark are laid against this to dry. But the tanner only wants the inner layers of the bark; it is therefore separated from the rough outer coating with its moss and lichen. This rough bark, the 'sole,' as the country people call it, is put

UNSTEAD FARM

THE DAIRY YARD, UNSTEAD FARM

aside for bacon-curing, and sells readily for sixpence a sack. When once alight it keeps on smouldering a long time. No kind of resinous wood, such as fir or pine, can be used for smoking bacon.

In a large farmhouse in my neighbourhood, now occupied by the owner of an extensive estate, the bacon-loft being no longer wanted it was walled off from the chimney, and had a new entrance made from a bedroom passage. It was proposed to turn the space to account as a cupboard; but, in spite of thorough cleansing and lime-whiting, its walls are so deeply impregnated with the briny infiltration that they have received from the tons of salted pig-meat that have hung against them for centuries, that the place cannot be used for any other purpose than the keeping of crockery. Everything of a more absorbent nature becomes damp and mouldy, and the place still gives off a faint, lingering aroma of the departed flitches. It seems to protest against being put to any other use, and to say: "I have been a bacon-loft for centuries, and I will not adapt myself to any other use."

In the same house is a fine example of an old farm kitchen. It is nearly 30 ft. long by 25 ft. wide. The two great beams that uphold the joists above are stiffened by three solid oak chamfered posts, resting on stone bases. The 'down' fireplace is raised on four courses of brickwork, and has the large iron hearth-plate that is more often seen further south, in Sussex. The middle space below the plate—in this case temporarily filled in with loose bricks—is handy for warming plates or keeping anything hot. To the right of the fireplace is a range of brewing coppers with their fire-holes under. The mouth of the large brick oven shows to the left, within the arch of the fireplace.

The great kitchen table is 11 ft. 5 in. long and 2 ft. 6 in. wide, giving room for twelve people. A big table was wanted, for in the old days the unmarried men lodged and boarded with the farmer.

One of the stone flags of the kitchen floor has, deeply cut

THE GREAT FARM KITCHEN

in it, the letter W. It covers the mouth of a well 10 ft. deep.

The dairy adjoins the kitchen on the side away from the fire. It is cool and airy, and there is a pleasant sourish smell from the tall crocks of ripening cream that await the butter-making. In former days this was the cheese-room; it is one of the oldest parts of the house. In the right-hand light of the window are two of the perforated leaden ventilators, of which very few remain in the district.

COTTAGES AND FARMS

In the wall returning forward to the left of the kitchen fireplace is the entrance to the cider cellar. Seven hundred gallons have been known to be made in a good apple year. Cider is still made in the district, mostly by cottagers, but a great deal more was made in the old days.

A small court or wide passage, leading from the farmyard

THE DAIRY

to the garden, is as usual paved with mixed material—brick, stone flag, and flat Bargate stone. Just across this from the dairy window is a granary-like building, whose raised floor is reached by a short flight of the steps of local stone that add so much to the pictorial value of these farm-buildings of the older type. In the former days of the farm's full activity this corner was known as the Iron Room. Here were kept spare shares and coulters for the ploughs, the heavy chains for loading timber, lighter chains for odd purposes, and a variety of the lesser implements of husbandry.

The picture shows the wooden barn-shovel for shovelling grain and the old wooden seed-lip for the sower. He carried it slung by a strap, steadying it with the left hand by the upright handle, while he cast the grain abroad with a round sweep of the right arm, that moved in rhythmical accordance with his forward progress.

This fine old farm has a grand range of barns, such as are only surpassed in massive structure and ample capacity by the old tithe barns built by the monks. They inclose the farmyard on the eastern and southern sides, the faces here most exposed to rough weather, for the ground rises to the west and north. A long stretch of cattle-shed is to the west, and a detached range of stabling a few yards away, on a higher level, to the north. The farmyard is therefore amply protected, though its large area gives it plenty of air and sunlight.

LEAD VENTILATOR

The main part of the great barn is 91 feet long and 22 feet wide, and in height measures 13 feet to the underside of the tie-beams. At the end, behind the spectator as in the picture, an additional length of barn, measuring 71 by 20 feet, stretches away to the left, forming a L-shaped plan.

Early in the nineteenth century, when corn was at a high price at the end of the great war, these barns were reckoned to hold £1000 worth of grain, to be threshed as required on the floors between the bays. Some of the last handwork by threshing with the flail in this district was done on the floor of the barn in the picture.

It was considered a matter of good management to store oats in the barn rather than in the rick. It was threshed out,

COTTAGES AND FARMS

a little at a time, by one of the few labourers who could still use the tool, and the fresh, sweet straw was tossed out over the rack-board to the beasts in the yard. They would eat up every bit; whereas, when threshed out by machine, the straw, having been put up in a rick, soon gets stale and

THE IRON ROOM

finally musty. In this state it is less appetising, and much of it is left uneaten and wasted.

The barn floor was either of stone flagging or of oak. There is one floor of each kind in this range, but the oak floor is the best, the stone tending to crush the grain.

Now, alas! these fine old barns stand empty. With much else that is gone of the beauty and poetry of agricultural life, the measured beat of the flail is no longer heard. Its cheerful, rhythmical sound is silenced; for the corn is now threshed in the field by steam machinery instead of being garnered and beaten out by hand, and the grand old barns no longer justify their existence.

The rickyard, with its stacks of hay and corn, adjoined the barn, for the produce of this great farm—for all their ample space—could not be contained within the buildings.

INSIDE THE BARN

But now the rick-settle, with its rat-proof stone piers, stands empty. On this farm the cultivation of wheat has almost ceased. Fields that once produced their eight, ten, and twelve sacks to the acre are now poor grass land. The very little wheat grown is not kept stored as it used to be, in the good days of English agriculture, on the settle, but is threshed out as soon as possible after harvest. The days of the rick-settle are numbered; as a protection against rats its purpose no longer exists.

COTTAGES AND FARMS

The rickyard is fenced off from the pasture by the stout old oak post and rail, good to see in these days of unsightly iron railings. It is the true fence of the country, and a thing of actual beauty in the free play of line of the rails and the slight inequality of the posts. A wooden fence of sawn timber must always be a stiff and soulless

THE RICK-SETTLE

thing; but for these fences the posts are simply shaped with the adze and side-axe from the butts of tree trunks of a suitable size, or of larger trunks quartered, and the rails are also of oak, quartered by rending with the wedge, driven by the axe.

It is often a matter of surprise and regret to me, when I see in large places, with hundreds of acres of woodland, what appears to be a thoughtless and stupid use of iron

26   OLD WEST SURREY

railings. These unsightly fencings are wilfully brought int
what is perhaps the most beautiful landscape, and alwa:
with disastrous effect, while the material for the mos
suitable fencing is close at hand and wasted.   It is usually

OAK POST AND RAIL FENCE

urged in defence of the iron railing that it is permanent,
whereas some day the oak fence must be renewed. But
it should be remembered that the labour of the not unfrequent painting with black tar-varnish—perhaps the ugliest
covering the wretched things could have—is also a per-

FROM THE RICKYARD

manent charge, and I doubt whether, taking this into consideration and the original expense of the iron-work and its erection, the eventual balance of cost would not be in favour of the oak post and rail.

And what a capital thing is the unpainted oak five-barred gate, with its stout top rail, thinning away for lightness' sake after it has received the slightly-curved stiffening

THE FIVE-BARRED GATE

brace. The gate in the picture, otherwise of a good type, with its correctly-shaped, slightly-curved brace, is faulty in that it has only four bars. To a critical gate-eye it looks thin at the bottom. The two top bars are rightly placed, then there should be three bars below that; these three being closer together.

The usual fastening of the older gates was a wooden latch, with the alternative of the iron spring, with upright handle topped by a knob, so easily opened by a man on horseback.

COTTAGES AND FARMS

And how pleasant, both in use and appearance, are the hand hunting-gates, and the oak stiles, with the convenient foot-board and the massive rounded rail, that by the end of the summer shows a bright polish from the friction of the labourers' corduroys.

It is sad to see, in place of these sympathetic, homely things, made in the place and suiting it to perfection,

AN OAK STILE

miles of dull and ugly iron-work from a distant manufacturer's pattern-book.

It is scarcely too much to say, that it is the almost culpable insensibility to the true value and rightness of these locally-made things, on the part of landowners and their agents, that is robbing rural England of so much of her priceless heritage of simple beauty.

There is no need for anything to be ugly, not even the

sewage-pump. Although its name does not suggest visions of beauty, yet it may be quite a comely object. Here is its portrait; just a common leaden pump, with the elm weather-boarded covering of local tradition, and with a wooden handle

THE SEWAGE PUMP

instead of an iron one, for the better grasp of a man's hand, and for greater comfort of winter use.

Besides the older farm and cottage buildings that show the timbered framing, there are others of probably the same ancient date that have the walls coated with rough-cast. The upper floor overhangs the lower; the roofs are framed of massive timbers. It is supposed that a good many of these may have handsome timber-work under the rough-cast, which was probably added later as a protection from weather, possibly as late as the time when many windows were closed up. There is hardly a village that does not furnish an example of some such way of building.

The pictures show two farms of the better class, seven or

FARMHOUSE AT SHERE, WITH WALLS ROUGH-CAST

eight miles apart. One has an ornamental barge-board of beautiful form and proportion. Both have evidence of windows blocked at the time of the iniquitous window-tax.

The backs of these farms are as interesting in their way as the fronts; the main house grouping charmingly with its out-buildings, and showing the inevitably good effect of local material used in the traditional way to meet the simple needs of the place.

Hurst Farm, Milford

The Back of the Farmhouse

COTTAGES AND FARMS

Inside also they are full of delightful incidents, though much altered—especially as to the fireplaces—either to meet more modern needs, or to gratify a perverted taste for a kind of sham gentility that would be unbeautiful anywhere, but that is specially offensive in its obtrusive variance with the quiet dignity of the good old building. But in many there

BACK OF THE FARMHOUSE

still remain the fine old oak stairs, with their stout turned balusters and well-designed string and hand-rail. One that is not far off has the handsome dog-gate at the stair-foot to prevent the dogs coming upstairs. The windows retain their iron fastenings, often of pretty design. Some of the older cottages have an iron spring arrangement, by which the casement is held in place when set open at any point that may be desired.

A fine old pattern of drop-handle, with a spindle that

passed through a door and lifted a latch on the other side, was not unfrequent.

The excellent architecture of the early seventeenth cen-

A Dog-Gate

tury is well shown by Wyatt's Almshouses, near Godalming. Here are ten lodgings for poor couples under one straight ridge, only broken by the transverse roofing of the chapel in the middle.

Iron Drop-Handle

Highly pictorial are the old tile-hung granaries, set up on short piers rising from the wall of the waggon-shed below; the piers topped with rat-proof caps of stone or oak. How well they are arranged for loading away the sacks of corn! The waggon draws up by the stone steps; the moveable wooden

COTTAGES AND FARMS

step-ladder is put aside, and a man, standing on the platform, takes a sack on his back from another inside, who had wheeled it on a truck and placed it upright in the doorway. In the bottom of the granary door is a hole for the cat.

The water flour-mills are usually buildings of some

BACK OF WYATT'S ALMSHOUSES

antiquity, and nearly always of interest in some way or other. Indeed, the mere fact of the placing of the mill, with its pond above and its stream below, and the working of it—the water dashing in the great wheel, the sound of the old-time mill machinery, the constant vibration as of something alive (some sort of plodding, lumbering, good-natured, meal-producing monster, fed and guided and controlled by the careful miller)

—the pleasant smell, the light dimmed by the floating floury particles—all these sights and sounds and impressions make a water corn-mill a place where the imagination is stimulated to something akin to a poetical apprehension of the ways of the older industries that have gone on almost unchanged for a thousand years.

The mere fact of the change of level, the building stand-

Granary and Waggon-Shed

ing on the higher ground on the side of the pond-head, with the quiet expanse of water, and coming down below to within a few feet of the level of the rushing tail-race; necessitating some kind of steps outside; this in itself compels the builder to ways of treatment that can scarcely fail to have pictorial value. And when these old places were built, and the builder of each mill used the material to his hand in the local way, just enriching it here and there by some simple

THE MILLER

The Mill-House, Enton

means, as in the brick cornice in whose joints the polypody fern has found a home, and in the toothed string-course above; looking at the building one is filled with the comfortable conviction, that of its kind, and for its place and purpose, it could scarcely have been better done. The stone of which this mill-house is built is not quite the same as the Bargate

STEPS NEAR THE OLD MILL

stone of the sandy hills, though it is a product of the same formation. It comes from nearer the Weald, and is quarried in larger blocks. Especially with this stone, but often also with the usual Bargate, local custom decorates the rather wide or uneven mortar joint with small pieces of the black ironstone. The bricklayers call it garoting or garneting; there seems to be no general agreement as to the exact word.

It would be easy to multiply examples of the country's older buildings, especially of the timber-framed cottages, but a subject so engrossing would need a book to itself, and here I

BACK STEPS, ENTON MILL

may only give it a chapter. Moreover, such a book has already been ably done.

But I cannot conclude these brief notes on cottages without expressing regret that (as in the matter of the needless use of iron for fences) when new cottages are built, they should not follow local tradition and be built of local material.

HALF-TIMBERED COTTAGES, EASHING

NEW COTTAGES OF AN OLD PATTERN

A New Cottage

COTTAGES AND FARMS 43

It is true that the old cottages are often damp and ill-drained, and wanting in many matters of wholesome comfort; but that is no reason why new cottages of the old pattern should not

WALL WITH GARNETED JOINTS

be made sound and wholesome and delightful to live in. I may venture to state this as a matter of fact, for I have built three cottages that I am not ashamed of. One of them, smaller than the one shown, I lived in myself for two years with complete comfort and enjoyment.

CHAPTER II

THE OLD FURNITURE OF COTTAGE AND FARMHOUSE

It seems a strange thing that, in these days of general progress and enlightenment, the household furniture of cottage and farm should have become so much debased and deteriorated.

In the older days it was sufficient, strong, well-made, and beautiful of its kind. It gave a comfortable sense of satisfaction, in that it was absolutely suitable for its purpose. Many of the more solid pieces, oak tables, dressers, linen-chests and cupboards, had come down from father to son from Tudor and Jacobean times. They had gained a richly dark colouring and delightful surface by age and by frequent polishing with bees'-wax, and were the just pride of the good housewife.

Now, alas! this fine old furniture is rare in these country dwellings. It has been replaced by wretched stuff, shoddy and pretentious. It is even more noticeable in the farmhouses, where, even if a good piece or two remains, it is swamped by a quantity of things that are merely flimsy and meretricious.

The tendency of the age, regrettably prevalent in England, and shown in a straining after a kind of display unsuited to station, seems in some measure to account for this. Another bad influence is the quantity of cheap rubbish, the outcome of trade competition, offered in shops; stuff that has no use or beauty, but that is got up for rapid sale with a showy exterior in imitation of a class of appointment used in houses of an entirely different class.

The painful result is that the labourer's cottage and the farmer's house, that formerly had their right and suitable furnishing, and therefore each its own respective beauty and dignity, have now lost both these qualities, and for the most part only show an absurd and sordid vulgarity.

Here and there one still meets with people who have

OAK TABLE, SEVEN FEET LONG

the wisdom to honour their own station in life, and whose good sense and good taste has led them to treasure their fine old furniture, and to resist the flood of pretentious frivolity that has in so many cases debased the homely dignity and comfort of the farmhouse parlour into an absurd burlesque of a third-rate drawing-room.

Here one may still find in the kitchen the long oak table, measuring seven, nine, or even twelve feet, with one long bench or form fixed against the wall, and another, loose, on the other side. Four legs of solid turned work carry the heavy top of all but the longest. These have a third pair of legs in the middle of the length. The top rail of the frame is of solid oak, two inches thick and five inches deep. Often it is carved or bears a date; 1599 is the date carved on the one in the picture. The top is made of two stout planks, each a foot wide, with a narrower one in the middle, the whole width being only two and a half feet. The surface, though now polished, is rugged: the tougher grain of the wood standing up with an iron-like hardness. All that could possibly be abraded by con-

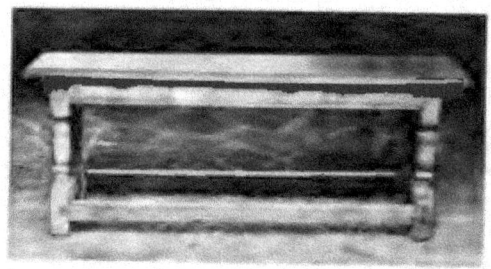

OAK FORM

stant friction has been worn away by three centuries of scrubbing. For in the older days the unmarried farm men lodged and boarded with the master, all eating together at the long table.

One falls athinking what tons of simple food these old tables must have carried—bread and salt pork, cheese and peas-pudding for the most part; and what thousands of gallons of beer and cider, drawn from the cask into capacious black-jacks, and drunk out of horn mugs. There were no plates in the old days, only wooden trenchers, followed by pewter in the best houses. There was a time, even before the wooden platters, when a thick slice of bread served as

OLD FURNITURE

a plate. Table-cloths were a luxury unheard of in the dwellings of working folk till quite a late date. All that was eaten from the table, except salt, was produced upon the farm.

The parlour table was of the eight-legged pattern with two hinged flaps. The tops were of all sizes between six and two feet, nearly always elliptical, with the longest axis the way of the flaps, though the smaller sizes were occa-

WOODEN TRENCHERS, FLOUR-BARREL AND SCOOP

sionally round. There was a good deal of variety in the pattern of the turning of the legs.

The round table with turned central standard, branching below into three curved legs, was in every old house, its form unchanged for centuries. Like all other house furniture these tables were originally made of oak, but exactly the same pattern persisted in mahogany when that wood came into use. The top was hinged and folded down against the upright; on being brought into position it became fixed with a spring snap. The tops ranged in diameter from eighteen inches to about two feet six inches; the one shown in the picture being of the larger size.

These three kinds of table were the most usual types, but there were other forms, some folding, some fixed. Of the latter an example of some antiquity is shown, with three upright legs braced together with a stout bottom rail. This was probably a children's table, as it is very low, its

Linen Hutch and Eight-Legged Table

height being only one foot ten inches. The common table height is two feet four inches.

Another not unusual form of children's table was made of a joint stool with a sliding moveable top. The joint stool was in olden days the seat of the carver at the end of the long oak table. The addition of the moveable top was of a later date, but as I have seen examples in Berkshire, as well as the local one shown in the picture, it may be taken that this later way of using the old carver's seat was generally prevalent. In any case, it makes a good-looking, little low table, with no appearance of irrelevant contrivance.

The top of the one shown is of one wide piece of elm, much warped. In spite of some stout grooved battens across the

Round Oak Table

Three-Legged Oak Table

grain, it has gone hollow in the middle; but elm, as the carpenters say, is always 'a bad wood to wind.'

JOINT STOOL

JOINT STOOL WITH TABLE-TOP

Carved Oak Linen-Hutch

Oak Dresser with Willow Ware

There is less variation in the design, and even in the detail of these stools, than is to be seen in almost any article of oak furniture. The one with the top and the one without were from different parts of the district, but show a remarkably close adherence to one pattern.

The three-legged triangular table was in the tap-room of a village inn. It is made of elm throughout. It is quite

ELM THREE-LEGGED TABLE

small, but gives ample accommodation for three men sitting round it, chatting over their mugs of beer.

In nearly every cottage was to be found an oak dresser, with shelves for crockery. The illustration shows an ordinary example. In some of the larger dressers in farmhouses, the sides that support the shelves are shaped in a sequence of upward and outward-swinging curves, so that each ascending shelf is wider than the one below it; recalling the bracketed posts and moulded beams, with floor projecting over floor, in the gabled fronts of the oak-framed houses. Some of these dressers have three drawers; others again are closed in all

OAK CLOTHES HUTCH

round; this arrangement forming a cupboard under the drawers, with a pair of panelled doors. In these cases the drawers were shallower.

The dresser shown, like many of its kind, had no back

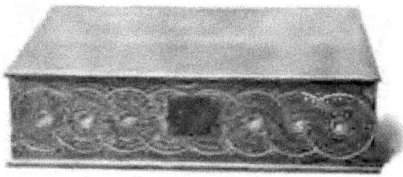

OAK DESK

legs; a thick fillet was nailed to a joint in the brick wall, and on this the back rested. It now stands in a new cottage; in its older home, no doubt, the top touched the underside of the joists.

Every farmhouse and many a cottage had its linen-chest;

locally called a linen-hutch, or cofen, a still older word. Some of the older ones are nearly five feet long, and were

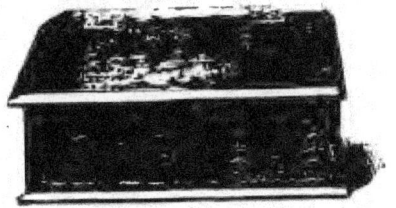

OAK BIBLE-BOX

profusely decorated with carving; but the average size was about three feet seven inches. The later ones had plain

STANDING DESK

panels with good mouldings. Whether carved or simply moulded they were in endless variety of detail, though in shape and structure they were on one general plan. Sometimes they had two shallow drawers at the bottom, and more often than not a fixed tray or shallow box, four to five inches wide at one end of the top, running front and back just under the lid for holding small articles, mending material, and so on.

Clothes hutches were much smaller and more simply

Wheel-Back Windsor Chair

made. The one shown is three feet three inches long and less than a foot wide inside. This is a well-made hutch; often they are much ruder. The ends are stout boards with a triangular piece sawn out of the lower end so as to leave two legs. The sides and bottom are simply nailed on, and the lid is hung on rough hinges. But it sufficed for the labourer's one change of better clothes, and meanwhile made a convenient seat.

From the older farms and small houses of well-to-do people there remain some of the oak desks and Bible-boxes, the latter generally ornamented with carving. Standing desks on their own legs are also sometimes met with.

The seats of our earliest cottage folk were no doubt boards with rough legs knocked into holes, exactly like the farm

OLD RAIL-BACK AND ORDINARY MODERN WINDSOR CHAIRS

hog-form (see p. 242); a low bench, on which the killed pig is scraped to remove the hair after being scalded, and, still later, cut up by the butcher. Another simple seat of the earliest type survives in the three-legged milking-stool, and a taller four-legged seat made in the same manner. This was refined into the joint stool, already described.

Some of the earliest chairs were of good joiner's work in oak, with high carved backs and ponderous arms. These were heavy things, and no doubt were meant to stand in their appointed places, and there to remain. Later came the lighter, moveable chairs of the Windsor type, also all of wood, with shaped elm seats and ash or oak frame and rails.

WHEEL-BACK WINDSOR ARMCHAIR

The chair with the rounded back is shown in the two most usual patterns, known as rail-backed and wheel-backed. It is admirably designed for strong daily use. The back of the seat has a projection, cut out of the solid, into which are fixed the bases of the two diagonal braces; their heads going into holes in the curved rail. It is a perfect piece of construction, supporting and fixing the back and making it absolutely rigid.

The later and still commonly made Windsor chair, shown by the side of the older rail-back, is without this, and though it is well made and fitted it is apt to work loose at the points where the back joins the seat. A glance at the two shows

RUSH-BOTTOMED CHAIR

the much better structure and consequent stability of the rail-back.

In the case of the wheel-back armchair this strengthening is not required, as rigidity is gained by the curved horizontal arm-rail and its many supports. The rounded shape of the brace between the front legs should be noticed as a clever way of keeping it out of the way of the sitter's legs. This chair has lost the upper part of one back rail, and has also been repaired with iron clips where the curved top joins the arm.

Probably the earliest kind of rush-bottomed seat was the low stool without back, such as to this day is used in Eastern countries. Why it is not used at home it would be difficult to say, for it is an extremely convenient kind of seat for many

Two Rush-Bottomed Oak Armchairs

odd uses about a garden and house. However, the rush-bottomed chairs that we know always have backs, the simplest form being the one shown on p. 59.

Two of the most usual patterns of armchair in use within the last two hundred years are shown side by side, and another of the same type, but with straight back-rails. This chair is of beech-wood stained black; the others are of oak, uncoloured.

The oak corner-shaped chair is of a not unfrequent pattern. It is solid and comfortable. The seat is not of rush but of wicker.

BLACK-STAINED RUSH-BOTTOMED ARMCHAIR

High-backed settles were contrivances for combining a seat with security from cold draughts. As a rule they have only survived in the older public-houses.

The benches in the cottage ingle-nooks were thick, solid oaken planks built into the wall at their ends.

Tall clocks, made during the eighteenth and early part of the nineteenth centuries, still remain in some of the farm-houses and even cottages, though the greater number of them have been dispersed. The better class of clock with an eight-day movement has the simply designed case of excellent proportion, with a plain panelled front and rather richly

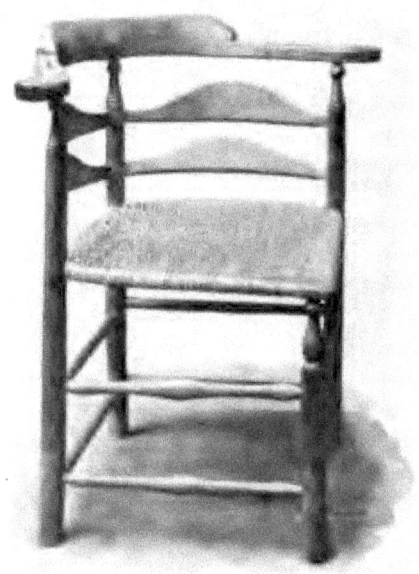

WICKER-SEATED ANGLE CHAIR

moulded arched head, surmounted by brass ball-shaped finials. The form is identical with that of the richly decorated lacquered cases of the same period, that were in the best class of house of the time, though the refined dignity of the best of these plain clocks makes them quite worthy of a place in any good house.

A cheaper clock with a twenty-four hour movement, but still with an honest oak case and works that would last for

A Good Eight-Day Clock

COTTAGE 24-HOUR CLOCK

some generations, was the pride of the young cottage couple setting up house. Where this could not be afforded, there was the capital Dutch clock, with its white-painted dial, ornamented with gay bunches of flowers.

The older bedsteads were of oak, with moulded and panelled head and foot boards. In good farms they had handsome turned posts supporting an iron-framed top, for tester, curtains and valance. In cottages this was commonly replaced by a light iron framework with slightly-arched top and brass finials. This frame was usually covered with a strong blue and white material in large stripes or checks, much like that which is now used for covering mattresses.

Exactly this bed may be seen in one of the pictures in that delightful book 'Dame Wiggins of Lee and her Seven Wonderful Cats,' in which the details of cottage equipment are shown with remarkable fidelity.

When I was a young child I had an old coloured copy

of this. It was already some thirty years old, and was then still one of the few children's books in existence. It may be had in a reprint—a careful facsimile that was superintended by Mr. Ruskin—price 1s. 6d., of Mr. George Allen, publisher, 156 Charing Cross Road, London.

I suppose that chests of drawers were very little in use in cottages till well into the nineteenth century; simple chests and hutches were all that had been required. But beautiful ones of richly-moulded oak joinery had long been in use in the better class of farmhouse.

A fine sense of decoration was shown in the brass handle and lock scutcheons, some of which (with the drop-handles omitted for the sake of clearness) are shown. The earlier examples were rather boldly engraved; those of the later eighteenth-century type were plain as to their surface, but endlessly diversified in outline. The ends of the actual handles, whose pattern varied very little, fitted easily into the rounded heads of bolts that passed through the thickness of the door, and were fixed by a nut screwed on inside.

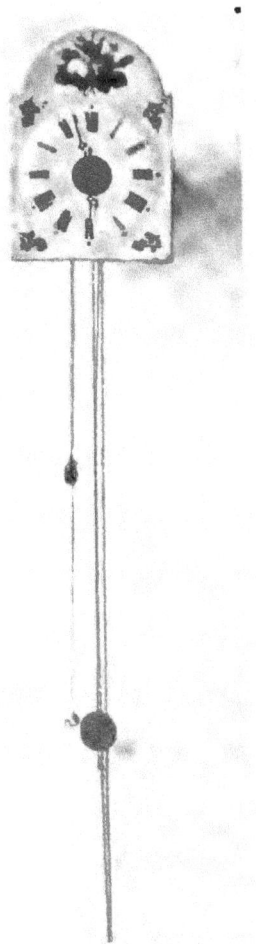

DUTCH CLOCK

I

OAK CHEST OF DRAWERS

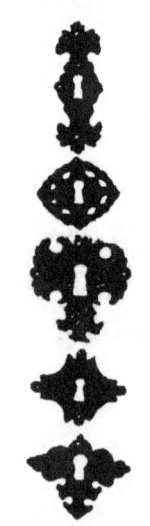

EARLY BRASS KEY-
HOLE SCUTCHEONS

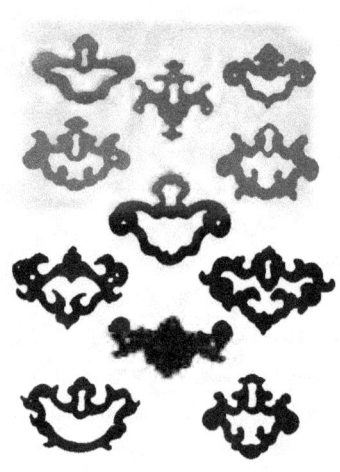

HANDLE AND KEYHOLE SCUTCHEONS

OLD FURNITURE 67

The old oak-panelled cradle of solid build must have served as the sleeping-place of many generations of children. It is of the seventeenth century, and was probably in use for two hundred years. It tells the same tale as the closely-curtained beds—of protection from searching draughts and bitter winter cold.

When the baby had grown beyond the crawling stage,

OAK CRADLE, SEVENTEENTH CENTURY

it was exercised and encouraged to find its feet, and at the same time kept safe from the fire, in the baby-runner. The upright rod fitted at the bottom into a hole in the floor, and at the top into a beam, or one of the thick beam-like oak joists that carried the bedroom floor. The child was put into the wooden ring, and the rack was arranged to suit its height. The child could then move about in as much of a circle as the position of the contrivance would allow.

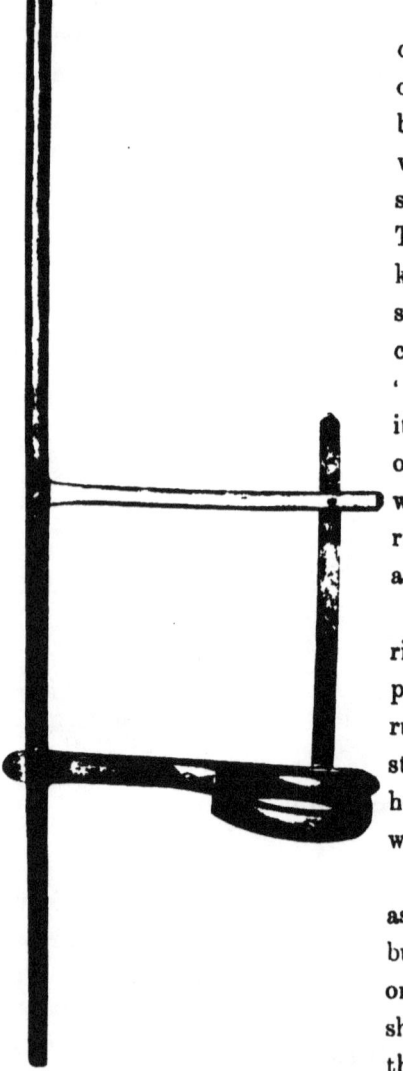

BABY-RUNNER

Among the smaller articles of cottage equipment, hardly of a size to be called furniture, but allied to it in that they were of oak joinery, were the salt-box and the knife-box. The salt-box hung close to the kitchen fire, both to keep the salt dry and to be handy for cooking. You may see it in 'Dame Wiggins,' hanging on its nail, just inside the opening of the fireplace. It was hinged with leather, because iron hinges rust so badly near the damp-attracting salt.

The knife-box hung upright upon the wall; its panelled front is the lid, which runs in a groove, and is drawn straight up. It held the buck-horn-handled knives when they were cleaned.

The knife-tray is the same as the one commonly in use, but the pleasure in simple ornament of the older folk is shown in the bolder shape of the heart-shaped opening for the fingers.

The wooden coffee-mill, also a smaller spice-grinder of

Salt Box

Knife-Box

Knife-Tray and Pewter Tankard

the same shape, of a hard, dark wood that looks almost like *lignum vitæ*, were in use in farmhouses, and, by the showing of the illustrations in 'Dame Wiggins,' in cottages

COFFEE-MILL.

also, for one of them, as well as a coffee-pot, appears upon her mantel-shelf.

CAT

This little book is throughout of considerable antiquarian value, showing as it does with great fidelity the equipment of a cottage in the earliest years of the nineteenth century.

The 'cat,' made of two sets of turned spokes, to hold a plate of muffins or something that is to be kept hot, sat by the parlour fire. Whether its name was derived from its fireside place, or from its way of falling on its feet either way up, seems to be an open question.

From the cat there is a kind of natural transition to the subject of mice. Home-made mouse-traps were in general use. One of these shown is so roomy that it would

LARGE MOUSE-TRAP, 10 INCHES LONG

be a comfortable cage for a small pet. It is ten inches long, and at any rate has the advantage, that it does not pinch

TWO DEAD-FALL MOUSE-TRAPS

the poor little captive's tail as does the common spring trap. The other two are 'dead-fall' traps, killing instantly by the falling of a heavy wooden block.

72   OLD WEST SURREY

An odd-looking contrivance, generally in use in farms in the olden days, was the bed-waggon. It is for warming a large bed, and must have done its work most efficiently. The one shown is three feet long, but they were generally larger. The woodwork is all of oak, the bent hoops passing through the straight rails, which are tied together with round rods. The whole thing is light and strong. A pan of hot embers drops into the trivet, which stands on a sheet-iron

BED-WAGGON

tray. Another sheet of iron is fixed under the woodwork above the fire, so that there is no danger of burning the bed.

This was probably a thing of earlier use than the copper warming-pan, whose well-proportioned hard-wood handle has a look of eighteenth-century design. The hinged lid, prettily pierced and engraved, opened back to the handle. There was an iron liner inside that held the hot embers, for these old warming-pans were always for charcoal or wood-embers, whereas the modern warming-pan, safer to use in all ways,

OLD FURNITURE 73

is for hot water only. Warming-pans of this class were as often made of brass as of copper.

Not many of the older implements of cookery, except some of heavy brass or bronze that will be dealt with later, remain to us. Nearly everything of the kettle and boiling-pot class becomes worn out and is thrown away. But one often finds things of the fork and ladle kind, some of them evidently of great antiquity, such as the iron fork and the iron strainer, pierced with three crosses. The latter may have belonged to one of the local religious establishments, dependents of the Abbey of Waverley. The brass ladle and skimmer are of a later time.

The iron skewers, with their original holder, are of large size; some of their heads form close double volutes.

The iron nut-crackers are big and heavy; they are ten inches long, and weigh a pound. They also look as if they might have passed round the table of the refectory.

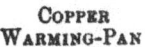

COPPER WARMING-PAN

The sugar nippers are much more recent. They were still in use within my recollection, when sugar was bought in whole loaves and cut up at home.

The iron snuffers and scissors of mediæval pattern go back again far into the past.

K

The iron rack with three hoops was used for cleaning the long clay pipes. When the pipes had become foul by use, they were laid in the rack and put into the fire, from which after a time they came out perfectly white and clean.

The box-iron has a brass case, with a door at the back to

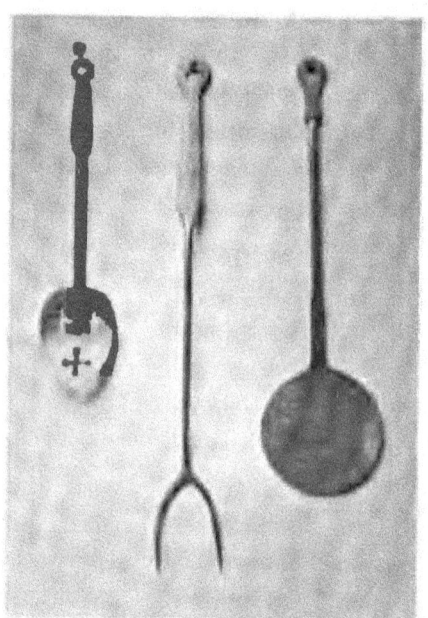

SOME VERY OLD KITCHEN IMPLEMENTS

allow a heated iron that just fitted to be put in. The ironing stand is a pretty piece of work, with dainty scroll feet and fretted edges to the parts on which the iron rests. The whole make of it shows the workman's pleasure in the fashioning of a thing that shall be of beauty as well as of use.

The wicker bird-cage is still made, though not so often

BRASS LADLE AND SKIMMER

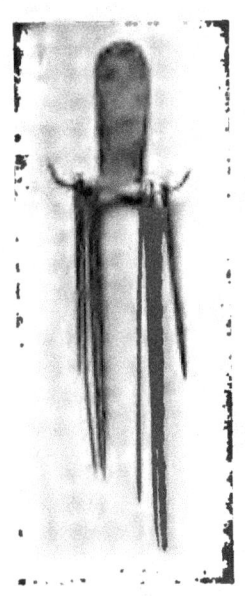

IRON SKEWERS

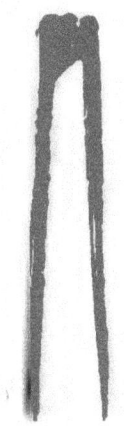

HEAVY IRON NUT-CRACKERS

SUGAR-NIPPERS

used as in former days. Just such a cage, with a magpie in it, appears in one of the pictures in 'Dame Wiggins.' It was hung outside the cottage porch or under any projection, and, when brought indoors, from a nail driven into one of the thick oak joists that in the older unceiled cottages helped so much to give character to the rooms. Endless were the uses of these joists, with stout nails driven in to hold all manner of things. Especially in the useful, roomy back-kitchens, where the great brick oven was, there were nails in the joists, from which hung baskets, tools, beehives, lanterns and all sorts of small tackle, besides ropes of onions, hams, chaps and so on. Everything so hung up could be seen at a glance.

The long-handled iron peel, for placing loaves in the oven and taking them out, stood in some corner close to the oven.

Very Old Iron Snuffers and Scissors

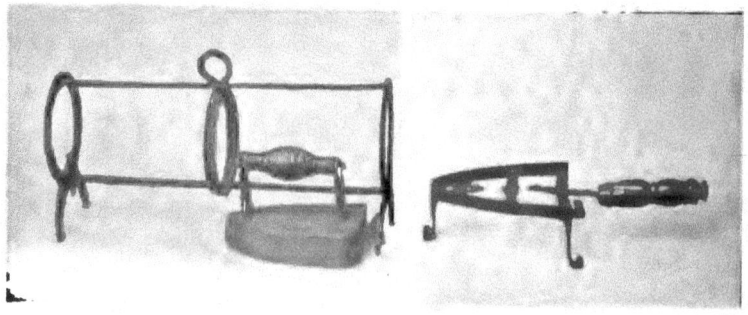

Pipe-Cleaner, Brass Box-Iron and Stand

WICKER BIRD-CAGE

THE BRICK OVEN

The older lanterns were generally of some size and glazed with horn. Pocket lanterns, glazed with mica, were also used. These were ingeniously made so as to fold flat and slip into the thin sheet-iron case, which had also a compartment for the candle. Lanterns were much more needed in the older days for people who were abroad after dark, for roads were much worse kept, and deep ruts and holes full of water offered many a pitfall to the unwary or unlighted wayfarer.

The barbarous room lantern with its many great eyes throwing out shafts of light, so terrifying to a nervous child, is happily a thing of the past.

OVEN PEEL

POCKET LANTERN

CHAPTER III

THE COTTAGE FIRESIDE

THE home life of farm and cottage, then as now, settled round the fireside.

Wide and deep were the old fireplaces, burning great logs of oak and awkward-shaped pieces split out of butts and roots.

A heavy oaken beam stretched over the opening, within which hung a little curtain of cotton print or of red moreen. This helped the draught by lowering the opening, while it was but a slight impediment to the head-room.

There were small niches in the wall, within hand-reach of the ingle-nook seats, made by leaving out two half-bricks, one above the other, in two adjoining courses; so forming a handy receptacle for a pipe. The old clay pipes had smaller bowls than those of the present day, and the bowl was set on at an obtuser angle.

CLAY PIPES

The simpler cottages had a chimney-bar or pot-hook pole, generally made of chestnut, and fixed across the chimney about six feet above the hearth, and hangers to hold the great iron pot.

Some of the older farm kitchens had that capital contrivance, the chimney-crane. The best of these, of which a good example is shown, show use and beauty happily com-

Cottage Fireplace and Ingle-Nook

bined. What a true artist he was, the grand blacksmith who did this admirable piece of work in his village forge. How well he felt where his material must go for simple strength and use, and when and where, having served this purpose, it might be drawn out into pure ornament, to gratify the eyes of those who should see it for hundreds of years to come, and to satisfy his own pride and delight in the doing of beautiful work.

The bottom of the upright is rounded and is set in a stone, in which it can work freely. The rounded top of the upright bar (shown free in the picture) works in a socket or loop in a short iron cramp built into the wall, so that the whole thing revolves easily in a quarter of a circle forward and back. The pot hangs on the hook, which can be raised or lowered according to the height it is to hang above the fire. As shown it is at its highest point. It might have been better had it been photographed with the lever nearly horizontal, resting under the sixth button on the quadrant counting from the bottom, instead of under the second. Then the smaller double turn of ornament that is fixed to the slightly-curved piece of bar from which the hook swings, would have come straight with the larger pair of curved braces attached to the quadrant, and the ornamental value of the bossy rivet between the two would have shown more clearly.

It should be noted, also, that this handsome crane had a third movement; the top bar forms a railroad on which the wheel travels, carrying with it the quadrant and its attachments; the square-built framework at the back alone remaining stationary. This movement allows any place over the wide wood-fire from left to right to be chosen.

The simpler crane of older work has only the one movement, that of swinging forward and back on its top and bottom pivots. In this case the pot was hung by a hook or a short hanger anywhere along the bar. Here again a fine feeling for beautiful enrichment is shown in the tulip with its leaves, and the twists in the square bar. It is

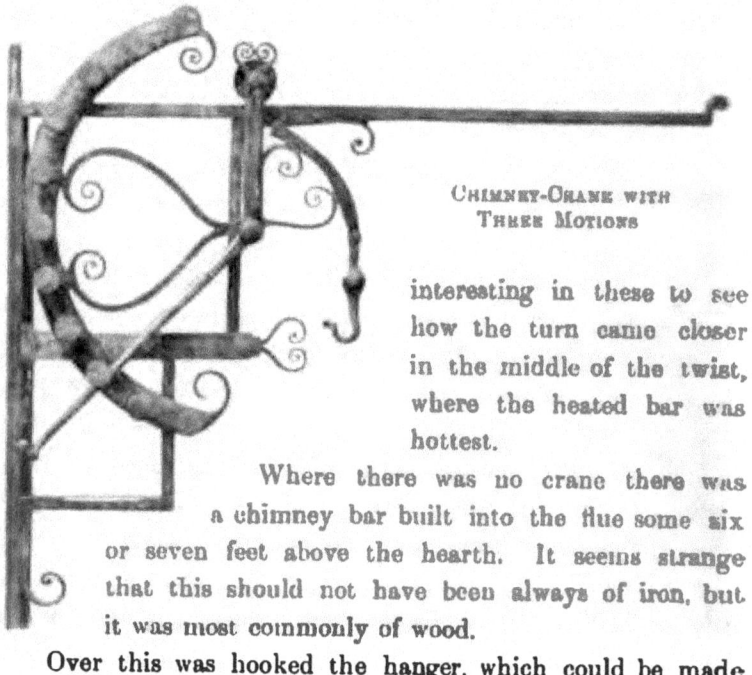

CHIMNEY-CRANE WITH
THREE MOTIONS

interesting in these to see how the turn came closer in the middle of the twist, where the heated bar was hottest.

Where there was no crane there was a chimney bar built into the flue some six or seven feet above the hearth. It seems strange that this should not have been always of iron, but it was most commonly of wood.

Over this was hooked the hanger, which could be made to hang higher or lower by means of the loop and ratchet. Some of the older ones, that may date from the sixteenth century, have a well-wrought *fleur-de-lis* at the top.

Through hundreds of years there was no variation in the general form and plan of these hangers, except that in some (not of the oldest date), the loop, that at its lower end caught in the teeth of the ratchet, at its upper end played, not in a hook-shaped ring, which allowed of only such lateral working as was due to misfitting, or the slight play of the top of the rod over the chimney bar, but round a knob worked on the lower end of the bar. This allowed of complete rotary adjustment, as will be seen on looking at the illustration of six hangers, where the two outer ones on each side are of this kind.

The chief use of the hanger was to suspend the great iron pot, or for anything of the pot, kettle, or girdle kind that had a hanging handle. Among these was the cheese-cauldron for warming milk in preparation for making the curd.

The old open fireplace was called the 'down' hearth.

CHIMNEY-CRANE WITH WROUGHT-IRON ORNAMENT

Iron fire-dogs were invariably used, both to give a little draught under the wood-fire and to carry two loose square iron bars that might be drawn together at any point to support a cooking-pot. The old word andiron was not often used, but brand-iron and brand-dog were frequent.

They were made both in wrought and cast iron. The small pair on the left in the picture were the pattern most common in the ordinary cottage. The taller right-hand pair are of wrought iron throughout, and have hooks at the back to support a spit.

The two simple cast-iron fire-dogs, of which the upper one, whose back-leg is lost, is of distinctly Gothic design, are of great antiquity.

The design of the other, though in any case of rude treatment, is somewhat spoilt by the two wrought-iron spit-hooks and their bands that clip round, that were added at some later time.

The wrought-iron cup-dogs were fairly frequent in farms and the better class of cottage. The branched top held

84 OLD WEST SURREY.

Two Very Old Hangers

a mug of hot spiced ale of a winter's evening. The back of the stem is a ratchet with moveable hooks for the spit.

Spits, besides the usual straight, plain ones, only a little flattened in the middle, were of various kinds. The basket spit would inclose a large joint, and the one with two prongs would also secure a considerable weight. These heavy spits have the grooved wheel for the chain that connected it with the power; either a smoke-jack in the chimney, or other contrivance.

The straight spits were kept bright, and formed a part of the ornament of the well-ordered farm-kitchen. They hung in the finely designed spit-rack over the opening of the

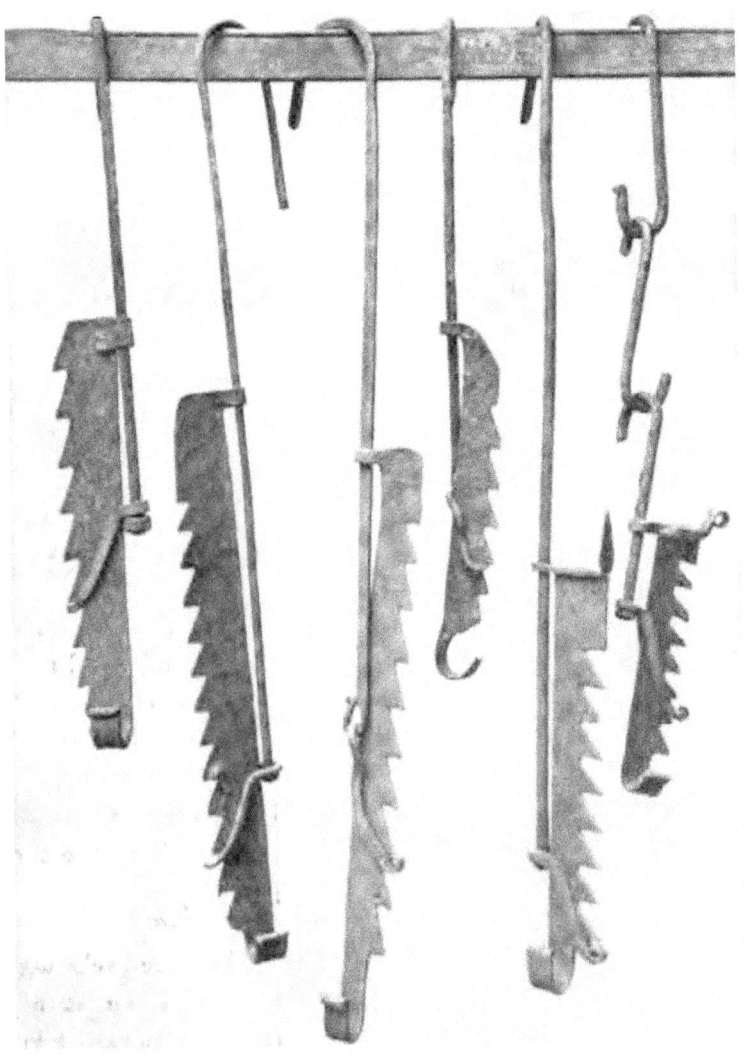

HANGERS OF ORDINARY FORM

hearth. The lowest of the grooves was high enough above the mantelshelf to allow space for ornaments, candlesticks, and some of the lesser table gear, such as horn mugs, brass pepper-pots, and pewter salt-cellars. The design of the rack passed boldly through the mantelshelf and finished against the ceiling with its own cornice returned to the wall to right and left.

There was sometimes a ruder and more coarsely-toothed rack, that held the keeper's gun or the farmer's blunderbuss in the same position above the fireplace.

Iron fire-backs were in general use, at any rate in farmhouses, but they were not nearly so good in design as in the middle of Sussex, where a class of back

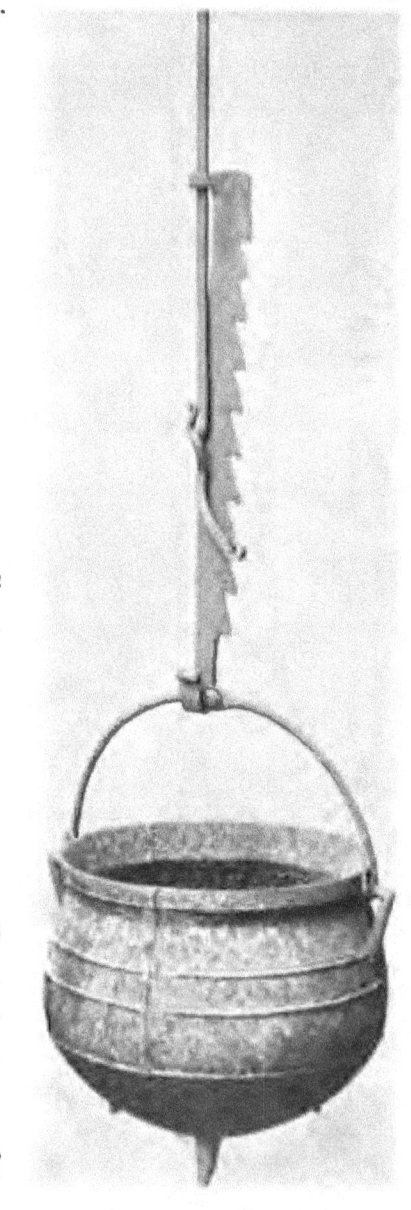

LARGE IRON POT ON HANGER

FIRE-DOGS

TWO ANCIENT CAST-IRON FIRE-DOGS

with very good ornament, whose subject is a great oak-tree with a royal crown and other emblems is usually very fine in style and execution.

I am quite unable to account for a handsome back, two

WROUGHT-IRON CUP-DOGS

separate casts of which I have known to be taken out of two old houses in the neighbourhood. It is evidently of French design, but I cannot hear of any record of its introduction; there are, however, several family names so well known in the country that one regards them as typical West Surrey names, but that are obviously of French origin. One can only suppose that there may be some connexion between the names and the fire-backs.

Basket Spit

The oldest cooking utensils that remain, other than the large iron hanging pot, which is still made in its original

Pronged Roasting Spit

form, are the heavy skillets of brass or bronze, or some neighbouring alloy of copper. They are solid, durable things, and I have heard it said that a great many more would have

90   OLD WEST SURREY

remained but that in late Jacobean times a quantity of them were collected and melted down to provide material for copper coinage. They appear to have been cast in one

Spit-Rack

piece, and they stood on their own three legs among the hot ashes of the wood-fire.

There was also another form of skillet that either stood on or dropped into an iron trivet. These must have been excellent culinary vessels, admirably adapted for that slow

CAST-IRON FIRE-BACK

FIRE-BACK OF FRENCH DESIGN

cooking that is so desirable. The large deep pan on the right is a cheese-cauldron, for raising milk to a certain

BRONZE SKILLETS

temperature before putting in the rennet that would make it curdle. It is made of thin brass.

None of these vessels bear any trace of having been tinned inside, a matter of some surprise to the modern

BRASS SKILLETS ON TRIVETS, SMALL IRON POT AND CHEESE CAULDRON

housewife, the more so that wine-vinegar, malt-vinegar (formerly called alegar), and verjuice—acids that we should not dare to use in an untinned copper—were constant ingredients in old cookery recipes; but probably these were only used in glazed earthenware.

THE COTTAGE FIRESIDE

Copper frying-pans had handles of great length; the one shown measures three and a half feet.

Iron trivets were frequent and well designed; the two shown are strong and heavy; good to last and not easily overturned.

Standing toasting-forks were of two or three patterns, the most usual types being those shown. The forks moved up and down, as well as round the standard, and were held in position by springs. Another toaster with a crooked handle, and a pin evidently meant for some revolving action, is shown at p. 278.

A toasting or broiling implement of another kind stood down upon the hearth. The shaped plate with the two half-circular hoops turned to any position on a loose rivet. The iron with the curved head was for raking hot potatoes out of the ashes.

Long-Handled Copper Frying-Pan

A small iron plate with very short legs and a rising curved handle also stood down among the hot ashes, and

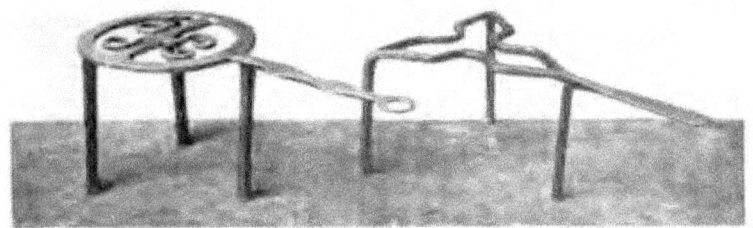

Iron Trivets

was used for small baking, or for keeping a dish or pot

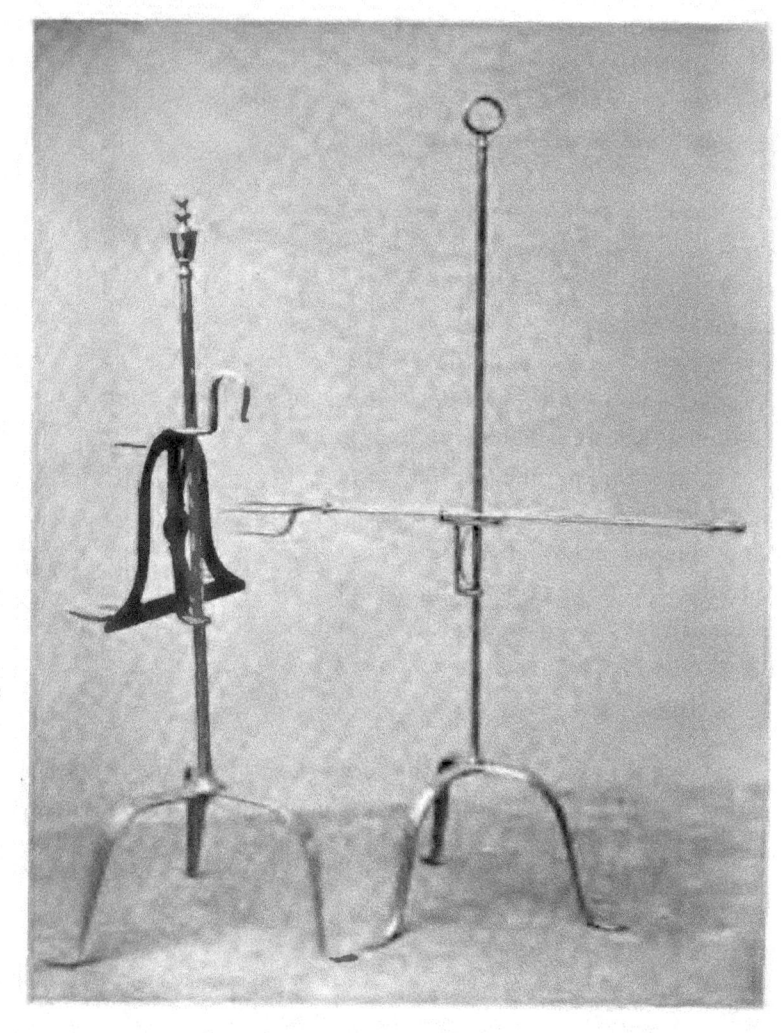

Standing Toasting-Forks

THE COTTAGE FIRESIDE

of food hot. Sometimes the handle was straight; often it was ornamented. An example of both is given, the one with decorated handle at p. 278.

The older fire-irons were almost invariably of the patterns as in the picture, but the pan of the shovel has lost a little

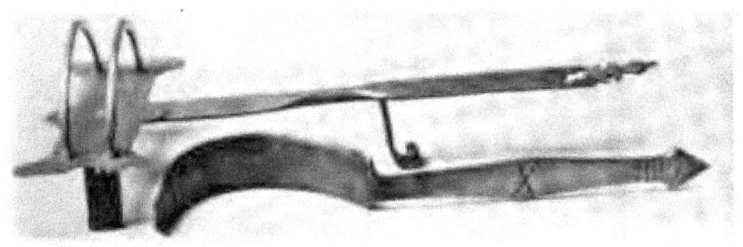

TOASTER AND POTATO-RAKER

of its length from wear. The bowed top or handle end of the tongs has an ornamental value, and in use acts as a good stop to the hand. Such a pair of tongs appears in Dame Wiggins's kitchen.

By most firesides was a pair of the small hand-tongs

BAKING IRON

called brand tongs. They were for picking up a morsel of live wood-coal for lighting the pipe. The projection was for stopping down the tobacco in the bowl. The nearest one of the two in the picture is the best-made pair of brand-

FIRE-IRONS AND VERY OLD BELLOWS

tongs I have ever seen. Its lines fill one with the satisfaction caused by a thing that is exactly right, and with admiration for the wit and skill of a true artist. For, simple country smith though he may have been, the man who forged this beautiful little implement had the hand and mind and heart of the true artist. The thing strikes one as perfect in proportion and balance and rightness of line. The ends that pick up the coal are fashioned into two little hands; the edges have slight mouldings, and even a low bead enrichment. The circular flat on the side away from the projecting stopper has two tiny engraved pictures; on one side of

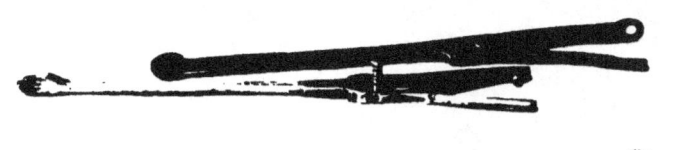

Brand-Tongs

the joint a bottle and tall wine-glass, on the other a pair of long clay pipes crossed, and a bowl of tobacco shown in section. The flat sides of the handles, and up as far as the shoulder where the plain shaft begins, have a 'purfling' of two engraved lines, one heavy and one slight. On the outside of the handle to which the spring is fixed is engraved the name of a member of a fine working family, whose relatives and descendants are still numerous in the district, with the date 1795.

Of about the same date must be the bellows with turned body and brass nozzle, on the left-hand side of the picture. The other is the ordinary kitchen bellows, that happily

98   OLD WEST SURREY

can still be had. The body is made of elm. The very old pair with a small body and long powerful handles (p. 96), I think must date from the end of the seventeenth century.

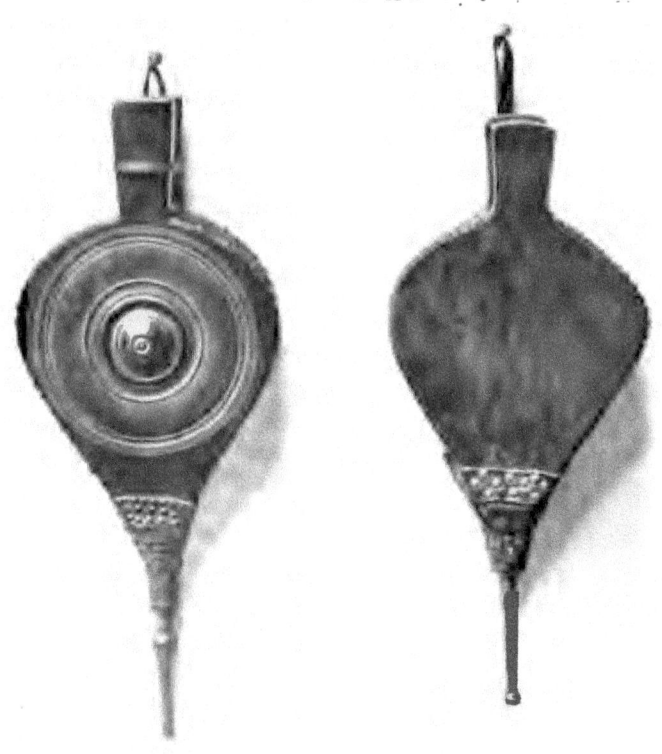

BELLOWS

It has lost the tip, probably one inch and a half, of its iron nozzle.

A kind of mechanical bellows is occasionally met with. It has a wooden base projecting backward into the handle for the left hand. On this is fixed by one of its edges a

THE COTTAGE FIRESIDE

drum-shaped, sheet-iron body, connected with a wide square tube narrowing into the brass nozzle. Inside the drum is a wheel with floats like a paddle-wheel. The spindle projects beyond the boxing, and has a small grooved wheel with a band connecting it with the grooved edge of another, nearly three times its diameter. A small wheel affixed to the axle of this one is again connected in the same way

WHEEL AND FAN BELLOWS

with the larger driving wheel, with its multiplied power, which is worked by the right hand. It is a neat-looking machine, with its bright brass wheels and nozzle, and body painted a quiet dark green.

A very simple and ingenious mechanical device is the kettle-tipper, or idle-back, or lazy-back, as some of my old cottage friends used to call it. The lower part of the hook by which it hooks on to the hanger rides astride of its upper

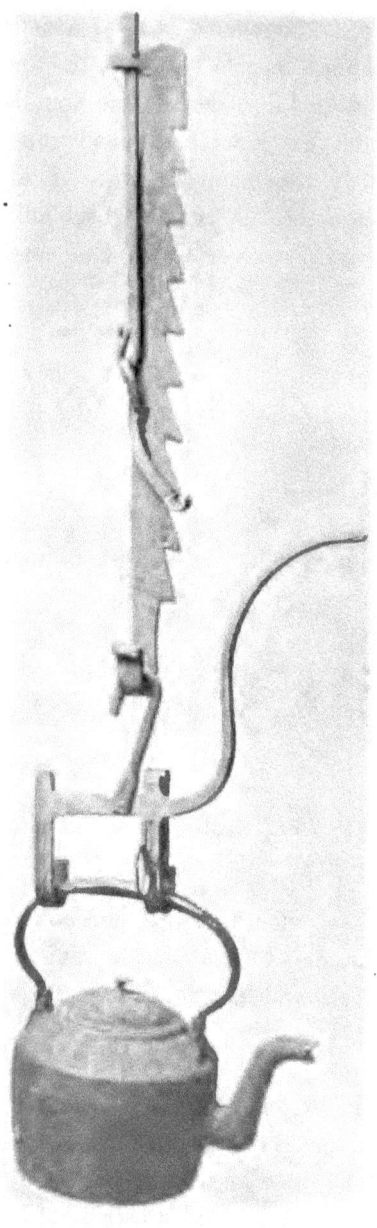

IDLE-BACK

flat bar and is loosely riveted, so that it plays easily. The two hooks hold the kettle. One of them is fitted with a spring clip, so that in the event of an upward jerk from a log burning away at one end and striking upward at the other, or any such mischance, the kettle would not be dislodged. The use of it is to fill the teapot without taking the kettle off the fire. This, as will easily be seen, is done by depressing the snake-shaped handle, whose form suggested to the smith who made it the little snake's head as an appropriate finish to its end. In the picture the kettle does not hang level, but it is in the position that it naturally takes after the first tipping.

CHAPTER IV

CANDLE-LIGHT AND CANDLESTICKS

In these days of cheap matches and lamps for mineral oil, one can hardly realise the troubles and difficulties in the way of procuring and maintaining artificial light for the long dark mornings and evenings of nearly half the year, that prevailed among cottage folk not a hundred years ago. Till well into the third or fourth decade of the nineteenth century, many labouring families could afford nothing better than the rush-lights that they made at home, and this, excepting fire-light, had been their one means of lighting for all the preceding generations.

In the summer, when the common rushes of marshy ground were at their full growth, they were collected by women and children. The rush is of very simple structure, white pith inside and a skin of tough green peel. The rushes were peeled, all but a narrow strip, which was left to strengthen the pith, and were hung up in bunches to dry. Fat of any kind was collected, though fat from salted meat was avoided if possible. It was melted in boat-shaped grease-pans that stood on their three short legs in the hot ashes in front of the fire. They were of cast-iron; made on purpose. The bunches, each of about a dozen peeled rushes, were drawn through the grease and then put aside to dry.

An old cottage friend told me all about it, and though winter was only just over, and the rushes barely grown, and she ninety years of age, yet, when next I want to see her, she had gone out and found some rushes to show me how it was done. 'You peels away the rind from the peth, leaving only a little strip of rind. And when the rushes is dry you dips 'em through the grease, keeping 'em well under. And my mother she always laid hers to dry in a bit of hollow bark. Mutton fat's the best; it dries hardest.'

Rush-light holders were mostly of the same pattern as to the way the jaws held the rush, the chief variation being in the case of the spring holders, which were the latest in date. In these the jaws were horizontal. But the usual and older pattern had the jaws upright, their only difference being in the shape and treatment of the free end of the movable jaw and the shape of the wooden block. The counter-balance weight was formed either into a knob or a curl. Occasionally it had somewhat the shape of a candle-socket. Later, when tallow dip-candles came into use, the counter-balance was made into an actual candle-socket.

PEELED RUSHES FOR RUSH-LIGHTS

The rush-light was held as shown. When it was a long one a piece of paper or rag was laid on the table to keep it from being greased by the tail of the rush. 'We set it on something so as not to mess about,' as my old friend said. About an inch and a half at a time was pulled up above the jaw of the holder. A rush-light fifteen inches long would burn about half-an-hour. The frequent shifting

GREASE-PANS

RUSH-LIGHTS AFTER BEING DIPPED IN GREASE

SIX RUSH-LIGHT HOLDERS

RUSH-LIGHT HOLDERS. THE TALLEST 9½ INCHES

CANDLE-LIGHT AND CANDLESTICKS

was the work of a child. It was a greasy job, not suited to the fingers of the mother at her needle-work. 'Mend the light,' or 'mend the rush' was the signal for the child to put up a new length.

Two pins crossed would put out a rush-light, and often cottagers going to bed—their undressing did not take long—would lay a lighted rush-light on the edge of an oak chest or chest of drawers, leaving an inch over the edge. It would burn up to the oak and then go out. The edges of old furniture are often found burnt into shallow grooves from this practice.

There were several kinds of tall rush-light holders to stand on the floor, both of wood and iron. The iron ones have nearly always a candle-socket in addition, indicating a later date, and the

RUSH-LIGHT IN THE HOLDER

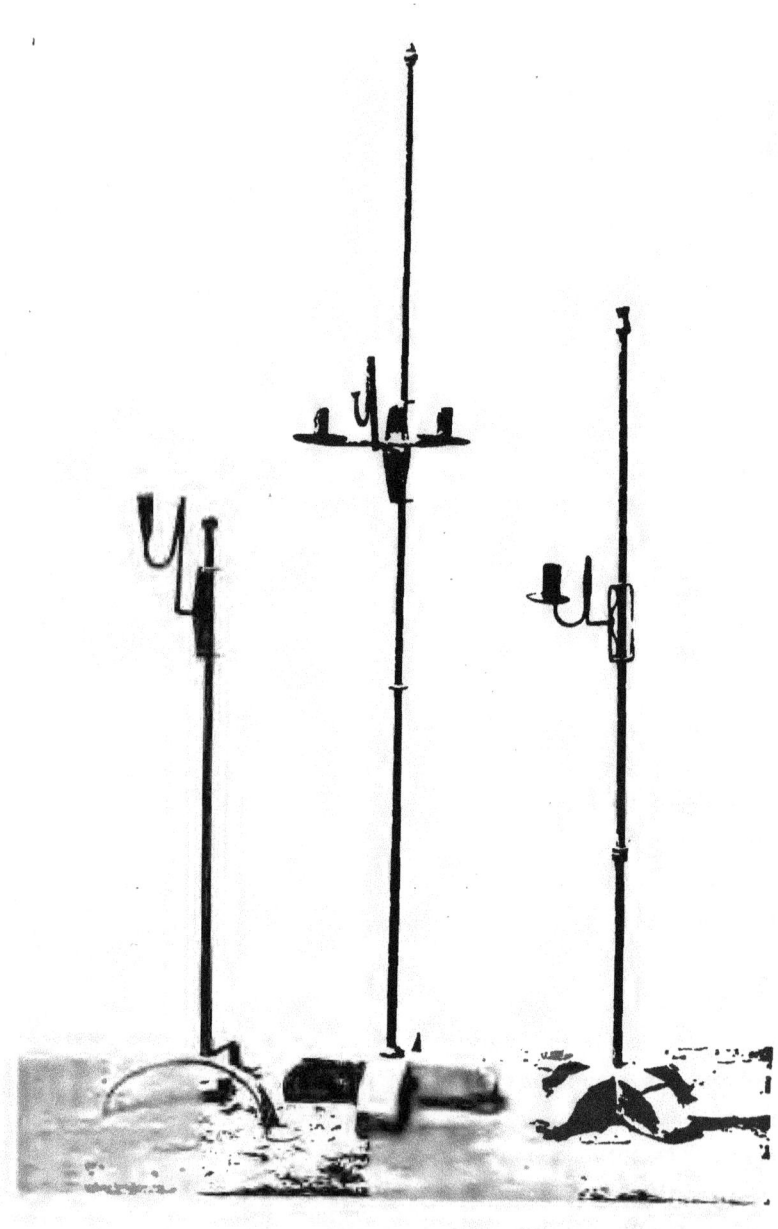

STANDING RUSH-LIGHT AND CANDLE-HOLDERS

same kind of spring arrangement to allow of the light being adjusted to the right height. Unless all of iron, as in the three-legged one in the illustration, they nearly always had the cross-shaped block for a foot.

The rough block to one wooden one is not its proper foot, but only a temporary makeshift. In this the standard is pierced alternate ways in each turned division, and the iron is shifted in and out. The other is a very old pattern, as may be known by the iron having no candle-socket. It works up and down with a ratchet and loop after the manner of a hanger.

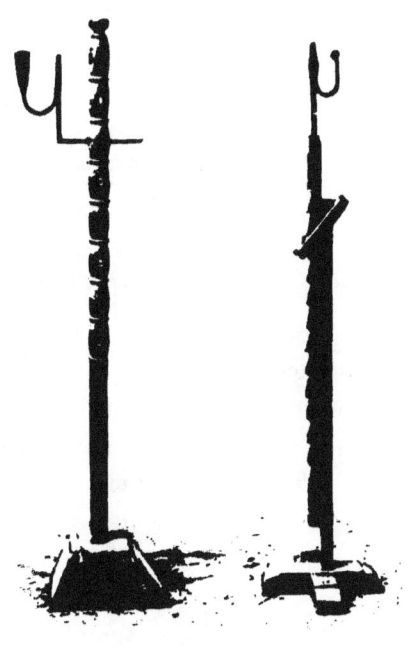

WOODEN STANDING RUSH-LIGHT HOLDERS

The only means of obtaining a light in the morning, if no red spark remained in the fire, was by the flint, steel, and tinder. Every cottage had its tinder-box; a round box of thin sheet iron, with or without a candle-socket on the lid. It contained a loosely-fitting disk with a ring handle; this was the damper to quench the tinder. The box also held the flint, steel, and one or two sulphur matches. These lifted out with the damper; some tinder was underneath. The fragment of flint was commonly chosen with a nice hollow place to fit the thumb, such as occurs frequently in its natural fracture, and a blunt edge for the striking part.

The steel was made of a good piece of metal, generally an old file. It was held over the fingers of the left hand, and struck with the flint held in the right. After a few strokes a spark would fall on to the tinder in the box; this was

IRON TINDER-BOXES

gently blown, and the tip of the match applied, when, if good luck were on the side of the housewife, she might get a light, or, on the other hand, she might have to try many times. The matches were thin slips of dry wood about three inches long and pointed at the ends. These ends were dipped in melted brimstone. A sluggish spark on the tinder was sometimes urged into activity by a tiny pinch of gunpowder.

SULPHUR MATCHES

Men in the fields would pick up a bit of flint and strike it on the backs of their knives; they had a piece of touch-paper in their pockets, and so got a light.

The tinder was made of cotton or linen rags—'Blue rags is the best,' one old friend tells me, but another said they used to favour the feet of old cotton stockings. 'You takes your bit of rag in the tongs and holds it to the fire;

when it's just well alight you drops it into the box and quenches it with the damper.'

A better class of tinder-box was made of brass, and has the same kind of straight handle as the good, simple hand-

BRASS TINDER-BOX AND BRASS CANDLESTICK

candlestick, also of brass, of frying-pan shape—a pattern that was widely used, for it was made also in silver.

'The first lucifer matches I ever seen,' said one of my old neighbours, 'was in the year 1839. They came from

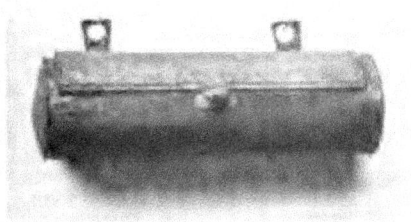

CANDLE-BOX

Southampton and were called Congreves, and were sold by the gross. I think they were made in France.'

An improvement on the rush-light was the rush-candle,

with the same material for wick, but much thicker, in that it was dipped several times in the grease, gaining thickness with each successive coating. These were the candles used in the sockets added to the rush-light holders. They were kept in the sheet-iron candle-box, which also served in later

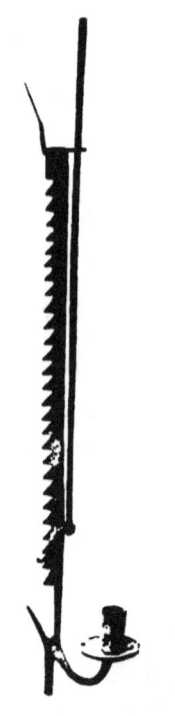

HANGING IRON CANDLE-
STICK

IRON CANDLESTICK DRIVEN
INTO POST

years for the tallow candles with cotton wicks of more modern make.

An iron hanging candlestick, with alternative arrangement for a rush-light, hung over the great farm dining-table. It had a loop and ratchet arrangement like a hanger. The fixed jaw of the rush-holder, an upward continuation of the

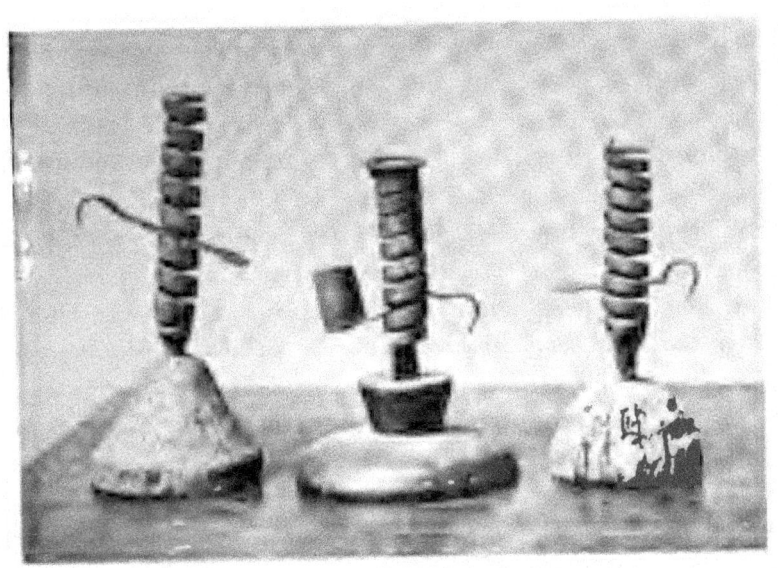

IRON SPIRAL CANDLESTICKS

IRON TRIVET AND KITCHEN CANDLESTICKS

lower straight piece, is wanting in this example. It has been broken off. These candlesticks were generally so hung that they could be swung up and passed over a nail or hook, to hang up horizontally along one of the heavy chamfered joists out of the way until wanted.

There were several patterns of iron candlesticks for fixing to a post or the joints of a wall by driving in the spikes at the back of the upright. One of these is shown. Another is just like an iron tobacco-pipe with a thick straight stem about eight inches long. The driving end is partly pointed and partly flattened horizontally, showing that it was meant to be driven into a mortar joint.

Some of the earliest candlesticks were made of a close spiral of strap-iron. The candle, as it burnt shorter, was raised by an ingenious device, whose action will be understood from the illustration.

The plain iron kitchen candlesticks were in use till well within my recollection. The iron trivet is of some antiquity, although it is evidently made to fit on to the front bars of an iron grate.

A candlestick with a many-jointed folding arm was sometimes made; never a very satisfactory thing, as each joint is a source of weakness. The one shown draws out to a length of two feet ten inches.

IRON CANDLESTICK WITH JOINTED ARM

Brass candlesticks of good design were made in the eighteenth century, and have come down to us with their edges only slightly and even pleasantly blunted by much polishing. The picture with five pairs shows some of most usual patterns. They were favourite chimney ornaments

CANDLE-LIGHT AND CANDLESTICKS 113

both in farmhouse and cottage, and were handed down with pride from generation to generation. The three pairs are of a redder metal—some alloy containing a larger proportion of copper.

The two pairs with the low-placed grease-plates look as if they might have been church candlesticks, though they came to me from cottage sales.

Snuffers were the necessary companions of the later

BRASS CANDLESTICKS

tallow candles with their thick wicks. The commoner snuffers were iron, the better class of brass. A very old pair of iron snuffers is shown at p. 76. The left-hand tray in the illustration is of a usual pattern, in rather thin stamped brass. The other tray, without ornament, is of a good simple design, solid and well-made.

Though not properly belonging to a cottage, a contrivance for striking a light, of which a fair number remain, may be

P

RED BRASS CANDLESTICKS

BRASS CANDLESTICKS

BRASS SNUFFERS AND TRAYS

mentioned. This is a flint-lock with a small pan for tinder, looking something like a stumpy pistol. Instead of a barrel it has a pair of short brass legs and a candle-socket. It is shown before and after striking. The flint strikes and throws open the hinged lid of the pan, flinging a spark upon the tinder.

 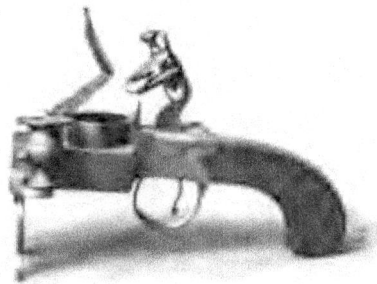

FLINT-LOCK FOR IGNITING TINDER

CHAPTER V

COTTAGE ORNAMENTS

THE farmhouse parlour, as I remember it thirty years ago, nearly always had a looking-glass on the mantel-shelf. There was scarcely any variation in its form. The frame had round pilasters, with caps and bases of a sort, running up to angle blocks, and on the upper horizontal part of the frame another such pilaster, connecting the two upper blocks.

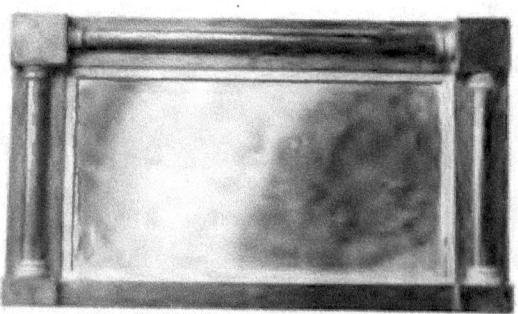

CHIMNEY-PIECE LOOKING-GLASS

This horizontal treatment of a pilaster was, even from quite an early age, an offence to my architectural sensibilities. Still, even with this defect, the old parlour looking-glass— also to be seen in the better cottages, was a far better thing than the cheap gilt-framed pretentious glasses that came after.

COTTAGE ORNAMENTS

The frame was sometimes black, sometimes coloured in imitation of some wood. The one from which the photograph was taken is roughly grained in imitation of rosewood, but the graining is so effectively done and the colour so well copied that at the first glance one is deceived. The caps and bases are either of stamped brass or of wood gilt. A gilt moulding comes next to the glass. The glass is thin, of a bluish tint, the silvering much spotted and blurred. But the thing has a distinct character and a date, the end of the eighteenth and the beginning of the nineteenth centuries.

It was made to stand on the mantel-shelf, the upper part being fixed to the wall by wall-plates.

The most characteristic of the mantel-shelf ornaments were the various figures of coloured glazed pottery and low-class porcelain. Many of them took the form of jugs. The Toby-jug was often seen; the figure an eighteenth-century farmer, with knee-breeches, three-cornered hat, flowered, long-skirted coat, and frilled shirt-bands. The old figure is extremely lifelike. He holds his foaming jug of ale upon his knee, and his face wears a broad grin in pleasurable anticipation of the refreshing draught. His pipe lies on the ground beside him—it shows in the picture by the broken foot—and his beer-barrel, much out of proportion, is grasped between his feet.

Toby-Jug

It is an actual jug. The handle is at the back, and the

forward cock of the hat forms the spout. The hat and the roses on the coat are of a dull purple, the breeches blue, and the patterned edge of the plinth a faint green.

Another favourite form of ornament, that at a pinch might be used as a jug, is the cow and milkmaid. The red and white cow's foolish open mouth is the spout, and the milkmaid is the handle. The milk enters by the top of her hat. Her bright red cheeks and smiling face may be taken as an attractive presentment of rustic beauty and happiness. These cow-jugs were in a considerable number of patterns. Of late they have attracted the attention of collectors, at least of the class of collector who buys old cottage things, because there is a kind of fashion that impels them to do so, but who have not much knowledge or discrimination. These jugs are now being imitated, and Toby-jugs also, and are sold as the genuine articles of the eighteenth century to this unwary public, that also buys with avidity, as the true coloured mezzotints of Morland, the frauds that are now being turned out of clever Dutch workshops.

Cow-Jug

There is a delightful *naïveté* about these cottage chimney ornaments: the proud young couple with their baby, the sentimental lady in the leg-of-mutton sleeves, the red and white dog, the cat splashed with spots of black and dull pink; the little house with blue roof and green door, and the heads of two children looking out of two top windows.

The Highland shepherd and shepherdess are better modelled, their sheep especially; some simple ceramic process giving a good imitation of the woolly coat. The shepherdess wears a wonderful sort of turban.

The third picture of chimney ornaments has again a house, with scarlet doors and windows and a mossy roof, evidently done by the same method as the sheep's fleeces. The pair of ornaments to right and left are flower-holders,

COTTAGE CHIMNEY ORNAMENTS

and are quite pretty things of white china with a raised white flower-and-leaf decoration partly gilt. I can remember when this class of chimney ornament was sold at country fairs, such as the yearly fair at St. Catherine's Hill near Guildford; the 'Catt'n Hill' of local speech. The same kind of ornament was also to be bought in china shops, as well as a better type, like second-rate Chelsea.

How well, and at how early an age, little girls were taught to use their needles may be seen by the samplers of the eighteenth and early nineteenth centuries. They have now been also for the most part 'collected,' but I know of several cottage folk who have the wisdom to 'hold by' their great-grandmothers' work, and who have resisted the offers of the travelling dealer.

PAIR OF CHIMNEY ORNAMENTS

Trees, birds, and animals, baskets of fruit and flowers, and flowery sprays are worked in coloured silk on a kind of open woollen canvas — something like a loose bunting; the treatment of the objects and the stiff border patterns suggesting an ancestry of some hundreds of years.

The worker of the pretty sampler in the dark wooden frame is still well and hearty, and to this day, in her eightieth year, is a beautiful needlewoman. The last line says, 'Ann

A SET OF CHIMNEY ORNAMENTS

Attryde her work aged ten years June the 3, 1834.' Most of these samplers have alphabets and numerals. Probably this good worker had practised these simpler things at an

COTTAGE ORNAMENTS

earlier age, and wished that her samples should be more purely ornamental. A verse of poetry or a text from the Bible never fails. The worker's signature is sure to be at the bottom, and generally the date when the sampler was finished.

The map of England is a sampler from the same hand;

SHEPHERD AND SHEPHERDESS

the counties are bordered in different colours. The portrait is that of the worker of these two samplers.

Fifty years before, Mary Madgwick chose the map of Europe as the subject of her sampler, finishing it in the year 1783. Her patience is worthy of admiration, for, not only is the map well worked and beautifully lettered, but one feels that the lines of latitude and longitude must have sorely vexed her spirit, as on the square-woven fabric it is impossible to work them evenly.

A sampler dated 1827, worked by Mary Ann Gill, aged ten, has the usual alphabets and ornaments and these verses. In the second verse the want of rhythm, relevancy, and cohesion must be forgiven in consideration of the excellence of the sentiments expressed.

> "God bless my parents evermore
> Who doth for me provide
> Let Grace and Virtue ever be
> My constant aim and guide
>
> For little trifles do not take offence
> It shows great pride and very little sense
> God's nature and good sense must always be
> To err is human to forgive divine."

SAMPLER, DATED 1834

The verse and signature in another sampler ran thus—

> "In thy fair Book of Life divine
> My God inscribe my name
> Then let me fill some humble place
> Beneath the Slaughtered Lamb.
>   EMMA SCULL, aged 6 years."

PORTRAIT OF THE WORKER

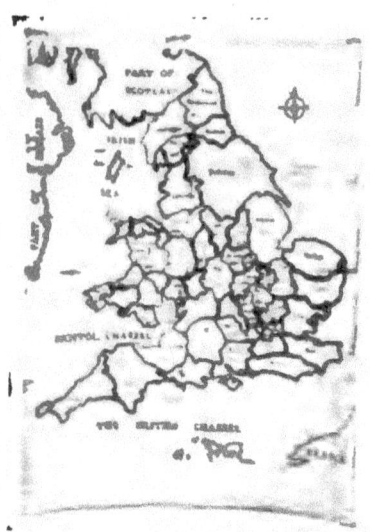

SAMPLER—MAP OF ENGLAND, 1835

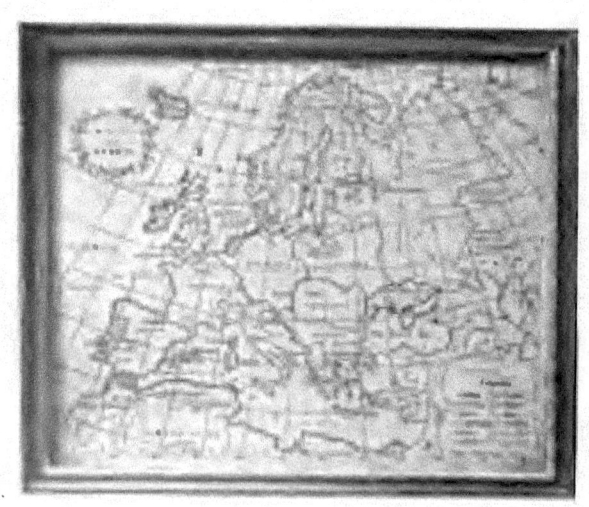

SAMPLER—MAP OF EUROPE, DATED 1783

COTTAGE ORNAMENTS

And in another—

> "Sarah Walker is my name
> With my needle I work the same
> And by my needle you may see
> What care my parents took of me
> My fingers they have taught me skill
> To write without pen ink or quill.

"Sarah Walker finished this work in the year 1814 April 1st. S. W. came to live with Mrs Woods at Rake Mill May 13."

SAMPLER

An old cottager now living in the almshouses shown at p. 35 has worked a number of curious pieces, giving a kind of elevation of the building, and a sampler picture representing her old cottage home. The return walls are indicated in a curious way. The tall tree or flower ornaments show a fine natural feeling for decoration. She was unable to get the proper sampler canvas, and these are worked on perforated cardboard. There is also some taste shown in the mount, which consists of a piece of pale blue-grey cardboard, whose colour harmonises well with the work and whose edge is neatly pinked with a half-round punch.

Another important branch of ornamental needlework that went on in nearly every cottage was the making of cotton patchwork. Some patchwork that I have of four generations back, whose date would be somewhere near the year 1780, is

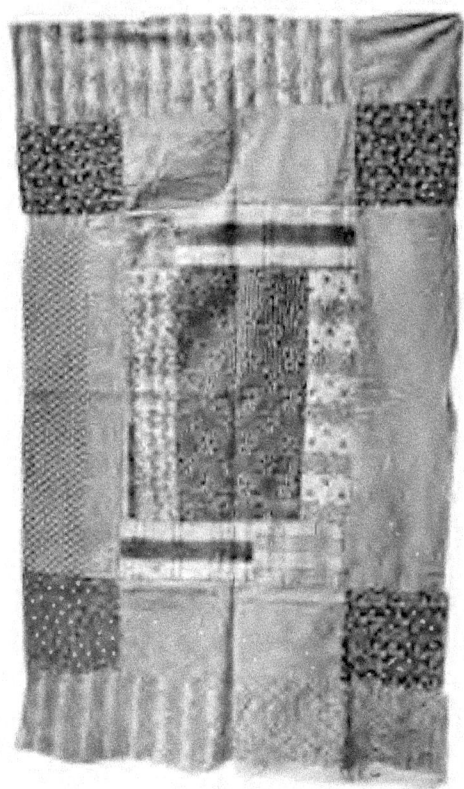

PATCHWORK QUILT—EIGHTEENTH CENTURY

interesting not only as an example of the work, but because it shows so many patterns of the printed cottons of the time. Some of these cottons, of low-toned purples, are charming and curious in colour, and the printing is done in softly-clouded bands that gives the stuff an aspect of rare refinement without taking anything from its simplicity. This

PATCHWORK QUILT—EARLY NINETEENTH CENTURY

PART OF A QUILT—PATCHWORK OF CHINTZ

piece appears to have been meant for the middle of a bed-quilt, but was never finished.

Another quilt of early nineteenth-century work has bands of the favourite honeycomb pattern; the little pieces

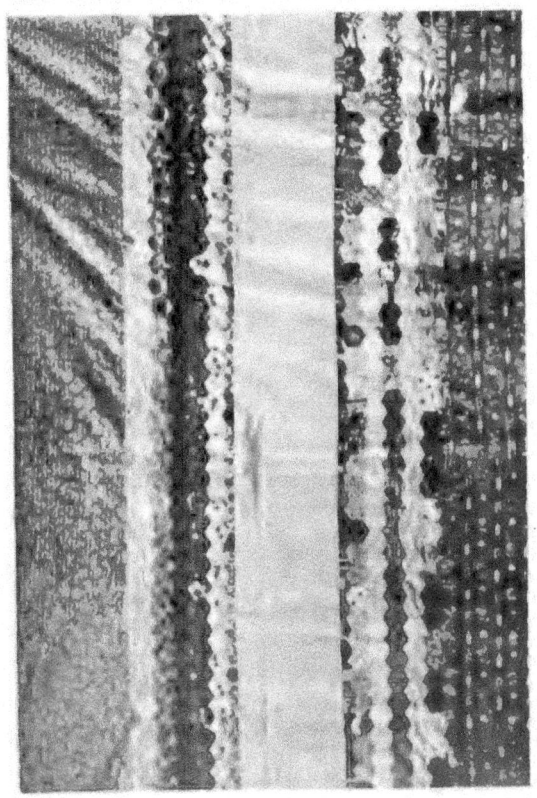

PART OF A PATCHWORK QUILT—EARLY NINETEENTH CENTURY

are 1½ inches across from point to point, with plain bands between. The outer, left-hand band is purple; the one to the right a pleasant combination of a deep buff or pale brown ground with the deepest markings of a dark chocolate

R

that tells as a soft black, and other colourings of purple, brown madder, and warm white.

A third quilt of gown prints shows a capital feeling, both for colour effect and for the disposal of masses. The nine squares worked together in the middle have all nearly the same value of colour-strength, and hold well together, in that they have a nearly common ground of dull reddish brown, something near the 'murrey' of heraldry. Of these nine, the four corner squares have in them some blue, which prepares the eye for the surrounding band of pale blue, while the murrey ground is continued in the inner three-sided pieces of the next band. The outer three-sided pieces have a general effect of warm white. It is really a white ground with a buff underprint, and a sprinkle of tiny pink roses with two leaves apiece, a green leaf and a brown. This tones excellently into the next band, an alternate criss-cross of buff and orange stripes, and a little figure like a flower in an eastern carpet, rosy and red-brown on a white ground. The outside is full of variety, some of the patterns of very interesting and beautiful colouring. All the pieces appear to be new, and the work seems never to have been made up or used. The colours are lively, but never garish.

The fourth large piece of patchwork is made of calendered chintzes; some of the pieces showing the roses, tulips, anemones, and honeysuckle of old English gardens, with patterns of oriental origin. It is a well-designed quilt, but would have been better if the band of white linen that surrounds the middle square had been left plain, instead of having coloured pieces patched on. The whole piece is so full of pattern that it would have gained by having the white band left free of the fidgety, irrelevant little patches. The next outward band, made of a sort of rose-pattern on a lighter diagonal square, with stars in the angles, is excellent,

COTTAGE ORNAMENTS

and the whole thing very gay and bright; fresh and clean-looking from the shiny calendered surface.

The cross-stitch kettle-holder, of much more recent date, with a picture of a kettle on the fire, is not a bad representation of a homely scene, treated in a direct and honest manner. The fender is green, and the red of the fire glows brightly between the bars of the grate.

Much older than this, possibly dating from the end of

KETTLE-HOLDER

the eighteenth century, is the flower-picture, worked in an application of pieces of cloth on a ground of dull white flannel. The auricula is strikingly lifelike, in two shades of brown and 'murrey' cloth over white; the anthers, in their natural straw-colour, being knots of silk. The strawberries are also very near nature; they are not merely cut out, but the edges are turned back, giving each fruit a distinct projection. The basket is of buff cloth; the pattern perforated. The spray of pansy to the left is of white and purple cloth, pencilled with fine slate-coloured corded silk. The tiger-lilies, very small in scale, are of orange plush. The leaves of the rose are of pale green cloth, heavily worked over with very fine worsted crewel of nearly the same colour; the petal part of the rose and buds are of floss silk. Work of this kind is generally done with a more restricted set of materials. This worker may have had only scraps, but the use of any sort of material that

PICTURE IN APPLICATION AND EMBROIDERY

was at hand did no harm to the work. It has the attraction of a thing that is perfectly sincere, showing the worker's delight in the things portrayed, and in the actual doing of the pretty, whimsical little picture. The auricula and the strawberries are life-size, the frame 11 inches square.

Where there were pictures in the older cottages they were for the most part of Bible subjects. The 'Return out of Egypt' is a small engraving of a conventional character that is not without merit, but that is spoilt by being very badly painted—apparently by a child. The two pictures of

The Return out of Egypt

BIBLE PICTURES

subjects in the life of Jacob—coarse mezzotints—are also muddled by very primitive painting.

The picture of the lady and gentleman, presumably on

Love and Retirement

their honeymoon, has for its title 'Love and Retirement.' The artist, wishing to show that it was a pleasant country

The Charming Florist

place, has boldly taken out the whole right-hand side of the room to show a pastoral landscape.

The 'Charming Florist' speaks for itself in its delightful simplicity. If the flowers are not exactly those of our country gardens, and if it should be observed that one hollyhock is painted with Prussian blue, these errors of detail are easily forgiven, for the picture is a perfect decoration for the cottage wall, and thus exactly fulfils its intention. Moreover, though its aim is but a modest one, it has that most precious charm of simplicity, a quality that seems to be almost lost to the art of England. I am told that

BRASS DREDGERS, PEPPER-POTS, SPOON, AND BOX

there is a companion picture, 'The Amiable Fruiterer,' but have not happened to come upon it.

Conspicuous among the ware of the dresser shelves, or on the chimney-piece among the ornaments, were the brass pepper-pots, and some of larger size that were no doubt flour-dredgers. With them is shown a handsome brass spoon and a brass box with two of the thick old George III. pennies worked in to form the top and bottom.

With the brass pepper-pots were sure to be a pair of pewter salt-cellars. Those on the right side of the picture are the oldest. Pepper-pots were also made of pewter. Of

COTTAGE ORNAMENTS

these, four shapes are shown, the oldest being the one to the left. The three pretty little brass spoons of tea-spoon size were also from a cottage.

The quite old cottages were innocent of inkstands, but there was an inkpot of some kind in the farm, always with its accompanying sand-box.

Various kinds of pretty boxes were in use;—work-

PEPPER-POTS

boxes, first of plain oak with a top tray for needles, thread, thimble, &c., and later, boxes of mahogany and rosewood, often inlaid with 'strings' of brass.

Tea-caddies were of good and often of graceful shape, with well-designed brass mounts, and ball or lion's-paw feet. When one considers the mass of rubbish of atrocious design that would have to be encountered if one tried to buy such an article now, one thinks with retrospective pleasure how easy it was to get a good thing a hundred years ago; when, if you asked for a tea-caddy, you would be offered such a one as the satin-wood box on the left

s

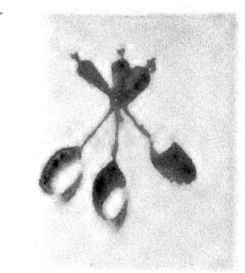

BRASS TEASPOONS

PEWTER INKSTAND

PEWTER INKSTANDS AND CANDLESTICK

TEA-CADDIES

or the plainer rosewood one on the right. Painted boxes were sometimes to be seen. The one shown has a dark-

PAINTED BOX

blue ground, and is painted with birds and flowers of an oriental character. The inside is red.

Money-boxes for children were to be had at the fairs

MARY SMITH'S MONEY-BOX

and china shops in many forms of earthenware and china. The one with a stem and foot is the only one I have seen of its kind. It is of coarse yellow and brown-splashed earthenware. On the face of the body is incised, evidently with the point of a stick, the name Mary Smith, and a rude figure of three trees, with the date 1837. Probably it was not made for any special Mary Smith, but was a pattern to be sold at fairs, where so common a name would be likely to fit some one in a rustic crowd.

OAK PUZZLE MONEY-BOX

The oak puzzle money-box appears to have been made by a clever carpenter. The picture shows how it holds together by the tight gripping of each edge of its six sides. One side is made slightly narrower than the others, and can be just released by the forcible pressing back of two of the projections. When it is put in again it is sprung into place by force.

I know nothing of the history of the pretty domino-box, except that it came from a cottage near my home. It

BONE DOMINO-BOX

is made of bone, with funny little hand-painted pictures of trees and houses, and people in the dress of the eighteenth century. They are on paper under glass.

CHAPTER VI

CROCKERY AND TABLE WARE

SOME of the earliest crockery I can remember to have seen in cottages is of hard stoneware, often dated, as in the case of the stone bottle or jug shown, which bears the date 1753. This is a venerable age for anything of a breakable character. I have also seen nearly the same stone bottle of a flattened shape.

The old mug shows how much the folk of four generations ago prized their household goods. The owner was a fine old blacksmith. When his mug had lost its handle, he made it an iron one with an encircling band fastened by a soft, tough horse-shoe nail. It is now a cherished possession in the family of my friend, his descendant, who has also a remarkable example of the old smith's skill in the shape of an iron tobacco pipe. It is of the long-stemmed kind, with the slightly-curved taper stem and a beautifully-shaped bowl. I thought it one of the cleverest pieces of forged work I had ever seen.

Examples of the same class of stoneware, but handsomely decorated, were sometimes to be seen in the farmhouses, but these pieces were evidently made for people of the squire class, as they bear their names and coats of arms. Two fine pieces of this kind, now in the Charterhouse Museum, are shown. The right-hand mug has, in incised lettering, the name Wm. Mott and the date 1726. On the front is a circular medallion with a portrait that looks like Queen

Anne, though the date is the last year of the reign of George I. On each side of the medallion is the figure of a soldier with a javelin; the other ornaments are a stag-hunt, with trees, and two rings of heraldic roses.

The mug to the left has the name Richard Tovey, and the date 1753. The front ornament is a square panel representing a feast; above it is a coat of arms, showing in chief a boar's head between two garbs, and a cross saltire with four bulls' heads. On the other parts of the mug there

STONE BOTTLE, NINE INCHES HIGH

OLD QUART MUG WITH IRON HANDLE

is a house and trees, a stag-hunt, and some heraldic roses. All the ornaments are in relief, the names and dates only are incised. The mugs are of a rich brown colour above, with a kind of mottled grain that has an excellent effect: the lower part is of a warm stone-colour.

From the character of the ware and its ornament these fine old mugs would seem to be the forerunners, at any rate in style and general treatment, of the excellent Lambeth ware of Messrs. Doulton and others.

The modern ware has unfortunately lost the characteristic

EIGHTEENTH CENTURY STONEWARE MUGS

MODERN LAMBETH STONEWARE

mottling, but the general aspect of the ornaments, though a little over-flattened, has been well retained; the farmer with his ale-mug and pipe, and his dog at his feet—in some of the patterns astride of his beer-barrel, in others seated on its head—the stag-hunt, the windmill and the trees, are all ornaments that could not be bettered for their purpose.

The picture shows on the left the large dog-handled mug, seven inches high. The pattern is a relic of the time when drinking vessels were scarce, and one mug went round. There are three of the dog-handles, so that, passing it round, three persons would drink at different places on the lip. The next piece is a tobacco-jar. Besides the cover there is a disk inside with a knob-handle, for pressing down the tobacco. Then there are the half-pint and the pint drinking-mugs, both with handles (a quart size is also made), and the beer-jug. The beer-jug is made in several sizes, both plain and ornamented. It is—and may it ever remain—the one best beer-jug of England. There is scarcely a good squire's table in the country where it does not have its place, and it is still used by many of the better class of farmer. But with that strange perversion or lack of taste, that neglect of the good every-day thing and unwholesome hankering after what is gaudy or meretricious or new, it is but rarely used among working people. In earthenware, china, and glass, the lower market is now flooded with cheap foreign things that seem to be put before the working-class public almost to the exclusion of the good simple things of home manufacture.

Another fine old make of stoneware that was formerly more used than now is that made at Nottingham. The two large stone bottles, seventeen and nineteen inches high respectively, are of this make. I believe that the left-hand shape, with the rounded shoulder, has now gone out of use. The smaller sizes of the right-hand pattern are still used for carrying beer to the harvest field. These large sizes were often used by cottagers for holding home-made wines, such

LARGE STONE-WARE BOTTLES AND RED-WARE LARD-POTS

as elderberry, cowslip, and currant. The round-topped stone bottle had been so used for generations.

This Nottingham ware is very strong and tough, and will

STONE-WARE AND EARTHENWARE PIPKINS

stand oven heat, so that capital slow cooking can be done in it. There are jars of straight and rounded shapes with lids, in a wide range of capacity; the best of jars for the

T

store-room; and pipkins, those excellent, cleanly, and much neglected cooking vessels. The second pipkin in the row of five is of Nottingham ware, those on each side of it are Lambeth; No. 4 is from Sunderland, and the fifth is of the common coarse red ware.

The two lard-pots between the large stone bottles are also of this common red earthenware, which is used as well for bread-pans and washing pans.

The old red-ware pitcher has, alas! almost gone out of

RED EARTHENWARE PITCHERS

use. It is a very rare thing now to see the pitcher going to the well.

The oldest of the four shown in the illustration is the one of roundest shape. It has lost its handle and nearly half its lip. It is glazed outside as well as in. The two outer large ones are the next oldest, number two being quite modern.

Here and there I have come upon examples of a round earthenware harvest bottle, but do not think these were ever in general use in the district. They are called Dorsetshire pills, and are or were made in that county. The clay burns harder than that of the common red-ware, it is paler

CROCKERY AND TABLE WARE 147

in colour, and the glaze, which comes down to the shoulder, is of a yellowish tint. It has always struck me that the name 'pill' may have had some ancient connexion with the pilgrim's bottle. These were generally flat; but a local antiquary tells me he believes it is only from the round shape.

The pitcher or stout jug, glazed dark brown outside and yellowish-white within, was from Sunderland or one of the neighbouring northern potteries.

At first sight it is a matter of wonder that so much

DORSETSHIRE PILLS

earthenware from the north and middle of England should have been in common use in early days in the southern counties; but it should be remembered that before the time of railways, there was a cheap though slow means of communication by canal barges. Another distant pottery, whose ware was a favourite in the cottage and public-house till well past the middle of the last century, was made at Bristol. This capital ware, with its excellent ornament and pleasant colouring of buff and yellowish brown, is now no longer made. The well-modelled figures of the cottage couple on the pint mug, and the hunting scene on the jugs, are exactly in harmony with the generally cheerful aspect of the older cottage life—a life that was hard-working and wholesome, and that had delight in simple joys.

The 'dipped' ware of Stockton was always a great favourite. It is not so often seen now in cottages, though happily the manufacture goes on, and it may be had at all the good china shops. The ground colour is a cheerful

GLAZED PITCHER OF NORTHERN POTTERY

yellow buff with a broad shoulder-band of white, and other white bands below. The broad white band has a decoration of a kind of tree pattern, made by letting a little colouring matter run on the ground. The ornament is blue on one side of the jug and brown on the other. The dark lines are dark brown. The whole combination of colour is excellent. The largest jug in the picture is $10\frac{1}{2}$ inches high and holds a gallon. It has a convenient projection half-way down under the spout that is laid hold of by the left hand, for when full it is too heavy to manage by the handle alone.

BRISTOL WARE

THREE JUGS OF DIPPED WARE

COLOURED MUGS FROM THE NORTHERN POTTERIES

In the picture of six mugs, three of them, namely, Nos. 1, 3, and 5 are of the same ware. All these kinds were formerly in common use in the cottages, farms, and public-houses. They are all from the northern potteries. Their pretty colouring, never garish or inharmonious, gave them a distinctly ornamental value on the kitchen dresser.

The dipped-ware mug to the left is of the usual warm buff yellow. On this is a white band with green trees, bordered with a brown line at top and bottom. The next is a white pint-mug striped and banded with warm brown black. The third mug has a white ground and a broad pale brown band with black trees. Above this is a half-inch band of blue, and there are two pairs of black rings above and below. The fourth is a white pint-mug, closely banded with black and blue. No. 5 is a pint-mug, beautifully coloured. The main middle space is a pale sage green with faint trees of a darker tint of the same, and it has a blue band in excellent harmony above and below. The last mug is buff yellow, with white and blue stripes.

In the picture of mugs and jugs, the covered basin and the one inverted are of the same pretty dipped ware; buff with cream-white band, decorated with blue ornament; the small mug standing on the inverted larger one is of the Staffordshire 'sponge' ware. Of the three on the box the left-hand little jug is blue and white; the middle one is ribbed and of a beautiful rich green colour. The right-hand jug I cannot account for. It has the appearance of considerable age: the surface is bluntly reeded and the colour is whitish green of the *celadon* class, with a high glaze.

There was a quantity of painted ware, such as the jug on the right, known as the Dutch shape; some of the painting

CROCKERY AND TABLE WARE 151

also with a mixture of a copper lustre; the ornament is of Chinese origin much debased. In some cases the painting is quite without form or sense, and yet has a certain decorative value.

Formerly the favourite pattern of dinner plates and dishes was the always delightful Willow pattern, that capital adaptation of the traditional Chinese design. It is shown on a cottage dresser at page 52. The most usual alternative was the landscape pattern, also blue upon white. This was

MUGS AND JUGS

made by Wedgwood, Spode, and other makers. The landscape, as on dishes and on the soup-tureen, has a river in the foreground and men in punts. A tributary stream is crossed by an arched bridge with a wooden railing. At the foot of the bridge on the right is a thatched cottage. In the middle distance, on the left, is a row of houses. Sheep are feeding on rising ground beyond the bridge, and on the top of the hill is a large building of vague architectural character, for it is impossible to make out whether it is a church, a castle, or a mansion. The tureen has the same design on both sides as well as on the lid, which also has a broad border of flowers. The handle on the top is a lion, mottled with an arabesque of blue and white; the knobs on the ends of the tureen are lions' heads mottled in the same way.

The teapot of the same ware has on one side a sailing vessel of very odd rig. On the shore in the background a castle is seen between trees to right and left. The other side shows a village or group of houses, with water and boats.

SOUP TUREEN OF LANDSCAPE WARE

There is a narrow band of flower design under the top edge and the same on the lid.

The pint-mug has a hunting scene, apparently in the tropics, for there are palm-trees, and, in the distance, very steep conical mountains. Three mounted gentlemen in white pantaloons carry long spears with large diamond-shaped heads. Their horses are prancing, and have long tails. The gentlemen appear to be tilting at each other, while two hounds are approaching a good-natured-looking large animal, whether lion or bear it is impossible to say, that half emerges from the flowery foreground.

Lustred ware was in great favour. A cheap kind was sold at fairs, but odd pieces of better make found their way into cottages, where they were greatly prized. The large teapot is nearly a foot long from spout to handle. It has a band of dull buff on the body, but the rest is covered with dark copper lustre. The small jug next to it is 3½ inches high. It is of a bright copper lustre with bands of yellow buff,

TEAPOT AND MUG OF LANDSCAPE WARE

almost the colour of yolk of egg. The small teapot to the left is very prettily coloured, with a cream ground; its edging bands and lid-knob are of lustre, and there are flowers of dull blue mixed with lustre.

The teacup is bright copper, with a wide band of cream-colour divided into panels by uprights. The panels have alternately a diagonal trellis and a flower-spray. The teapot on the right is of bright copper lustre. On the body is a band of ornament whose ground colour is a subdued green; on this are white flowers in relief edged with red, and leaves of a paler green. The lid has also a green band.

Pieces of the black ware made by Wedgwood were also occasionally to be found in cottages; they were probably single

VARIOUS PIECES OF LUSTRE WARE

pieces (of which the other portions of a set were broken), given away as of little value.

Jugs of a white Staffordshire ware, decorated with trophies

BLACK WEDGWOOD WARE

of agricultural implements, were favourites in farmhouses in the early part of the nineteenth century. The one shown is preserved as a precious relic in a fine old farm. It has lost its handle, and a sheet-iron one has been carefully fitted in its place, and is fixed with leaden rivets.

The implements, &c., on the face shown are, in the middle, a plough, and on either side of it a sheaf and a milking-pail. Above are a hay-fork and hay-rake and the three-pronged wooden fork, which was formerly also used in hay-making, with something that may be a flail or a hay-knife, to fill up

FARM-JUG OF STAFFORDSHIRE WARE

the left-hand space. As the group near it, connected by a ribbon, are all haying tools, it is probably the great broad-bladed knife for cutting the hay out of the stack. Below the plough are an axe and a mattock crossed. On a ribbon above is the good old agricultural motto 'God speed the Plow,' and below, the lines—

> He that by the Plow would thrive
> Himself must either hold or Drive.

The other side of the jug is also ornamented with a circle enclosing this verse, surrounded by a device of implements—

Success
to the plough
The fleece and the Pail
May the Landlord
Ever Flourish
And the Tenant
never fail

In the upper part of the encircling ornament are a spade and a digging-fork; to the left, a scythe and a dung-drag; to the right, axe, sickle, and flail; at the bottom, the stilts of a plough, a hay-rake, fork, and two sheaves.

The tools themselves are interesting, showing the older forms; the hay-rake of the pattern that has the curved stiffening brace passing through the handle and into the head of the rake. The design is structurally good except that the handle

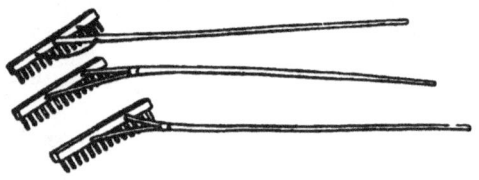

THREE PATTERNS OF HAY-RAKE

is weakened near the head, where it is bored for the brace to pass through, and it is a shade heavier than the later tool, in which the handle itself is split and parted. I think the modern tool is the better one, especially the Kentish shape—the middle one of the three shown—in which the handle is a little bowed upwards before it meets the head.

The sickle, with its toothed edge, is clearly shown. It should not be confounded with the reaping-hook, nor with the fag-hook. The differences between these tools will be described elsewhere.

CHAPTER VII

HOME INDUSTRIES

It is so long since the spinning-wheel was at work in this district that I cannot hear of any one in the neighbourhood who remembers having seen it used, although some of my old friends among the labouring folk are between eighty and ninety years of age. But the old implements remain, coming to light from time to time when a farm or yeoman's dwelling changes hands, and the barely-lighted loft over the bedroom floor, that has been the receptacle for lumber for generations, is cleared out.

Many of these lofts have been safe repositories for articles that for a time were merely useless encumbrances, but that now have acquired an antiquarian value. Spinning and winding wheels have come out of them, none the worse for their many years of retirement and thick coatings of dust and cobwebs.

When they are carefully cleaned, one cannot but admire their simple structure, and the way their makers delighted in putting pretty turned work into their legs and into the many spindles that went to form their structure.

The sight of these simple pieces of mechanism—mechanism that supplemented but did not supplant hand labour—makes one think how much fuller and more interesting was the rural home life of the older days, when nearly everything for daily use and daily food was made and produced on the farm or in the immediate district; when people found their joy in

SPINNING-WHEEL

THE WINDER

life at home, instead of frittering away half their time in looking for it somewhere else; when they honoured their own state of life by making the best of it within its own good limits, instead of tormenting themselves with a restless striving to be, or at any rate to appear to be, something that they are not. Surely that older life was better and happier and more fruitful, and even, I venture to assume, much fuller of sane and wholesome daily interests.

Surely it is more interesting, and the thing when made of a more vital value, when it is made at home from the very beginning, than when it is bought at a shop.

Look at the picture of the little silk-winder. Perhaps

A Silk-Winder

it belonged, a hundred years ago, to some squire's wife or daughter. She was possibly doing a piece of that pretty old work where a soft narrow silk ribbon is gathered up into little flowers. She wanted some yards of ribbon of a golden colour, something like oat-straw. Nothing of the kind was to be had in the market-town, and she had seen nobody of late likely to be going to London, who could do her commission. So she kept some silk-worms, and when they had done their work she wound off the silken thread from the cocoons on this little winder—a few cocoons at a time bobbing about in a basin of lukewarm water. Then she would wind it off from the dainty hank that had gathered round the pegs of the extended arms, on to the little spools, till she had enough on them to form the threads of the warp and a reserve for the tiny shuttle. And then she had a little loom, home-made—I made one myself once—and wove her golden ribbon.

You may fancy how carefully she used the ribbon: working it in without wasting a quarter of an inch!

Straw-plaiting was done in the cottages in the early part of the nineteenth century, no doubt set going by William Cobbett, who was born near Farnham, and, though his home was in Hampshire, was a frequent visitor to the district during his many rides to observe the state of agriculture of the home counties. To prepare the straw for the work it had to be flattened by being pressed through a hand-roller. The roller, which has a beechwood frame and a pair of hardwood rollers, was fixed upright to the edge of a table by means of a wooden screw that passed through the table from below upwards. The head part of the screw is missing, but its end shows, passing through the lower of the two under-braces of the frame and screwing into the upper of the two. By an oversight it was photographed on the wrong side, making it appear left-handed.

STRAW-CRUSHER

Country methods of washing clothes have scarcely changed: the old coarse red-ware pan is always a convenient and favourite wash-tub.

The shape of the smoothing irons has altered somewhat: the oldest of some cottage irons that I have and that must

The Red-Ware Pan

be a hundred years old or more, have very blunt noses, and the handles rake forward in a way that now looks unusual.

OLD SMOOTHING IRONS

But in place of the fine hemp cord that was the older drying-line. there is now a galvanised iron wire. The wire

THE IRON WASHING-LINE

has advantages in that it saves time and trouble, for once fixed it remains in place. The hemp line had to be taken

HOME INDUSTRIES

down; for if it was put up on a dry day and strained tight, a shower of rain or a heavy dew would break it by contracting it, and leaving it out made it rot. But the wire is bad in some ways, for, if the coating of zinc has any imperfections, there comes a rusty patch on the linen—an iron-mould; and if the stuff is old or tender, the wooden peg jamming it upon the iron will sometimes cut clean through it.

A COTTAGER'S BEE-HIVES

Many cottagers are clever bee-keepers. The old straw hive is still in use among the poorer folk. Luckily for appearance' sake, it is cheaper than the more scientific wooden one, and the cottager's device for sheltering it, as in the case shown, with a bonnet made of pieces of sacking, and the broken halves of a red-ware washing-pan, adds to the prettiness of the little bee establishment.

By local custom a wandering swarm, worth from eight to ten shillings, is the property of any one on whose place it settles, though of course it is not claimed among good neighbours when the one who hives it knows where it came from. But often a swarm flies far before settling. Any clanging noise is supposed to stop its flight and induce it to come down, and there was thought to be a special attraction about the noise of an old ploughshare beaten on with a heavy door-key. In the month of May, when the first

BUTTER SCALES WITH WOODEN PANS

swarms may be expected, there is often a spare new straw hive in the back-kitchen, and in the older days a ploughshare was also in readiness. The door-key was always handy.

There were generally some cottagers within a few miles' distance who made straw hives during the winter and early spring. They were bound together with a lacing made of thinly-shaved hazel or withy. Now they are mostly made by wandering gipsy people.

Wooden scales for weighing butter were used of old in the farms. The scale-pans hung by tapes; the beam was of iron.

HOME INDUSTRIES

The wooden butter-prints were of many devices, but the subjects most often repeated were a cow, with or without ornamental accessories, a rose or a forget-me-not, a sheaf of

BUTTER-PRINTS

corn or a twig of apples. The small prints, six on one block in the illustration, are beautifully cut, and are more than two hundred years old.

The fine old shovel-shaped butter-scoop is of a pattern still in use. The wooden spoon is perhaps a hundred years old. It is beautifully made and finished, and has been care-

BUTTER SCOOP AND WOODEN SPOON

fully preserved; it probably came out of some good house, where it may have been used by the ladies of the family in the still-room, according to the good old fashion of our great-great-grandmothers.

In old days taps for barrels, then called spigots, were

always of wood—farmers and even cottagers commonly brewed their own beer. Some of those used for large casks were a good two and a half inches across the wide flat end that took the blows of the mallet.

A cottage industry that still survives in this neighbourhood is the making of birch and heath brooms. As no cast-iron or machine-made substitute for these useful things has yet appeared, let us hope that they may still remain. Their safety is probably in their cheapness, for the price in the country, buying direct from the maker, is three and sixpence a dozen for birch and half-a-crown a dozen for heath. The materials cost the makers very little; often much less than the rightful owner of the birches and handle stuff intends or is aware of, and they are quickly and easily made.

LARGE WOODEN SPIGOT

Among the broom-squarers or broom-squires there have always been some very rough characters. Two generations ago they were rougher still, for then their haunts among the heathy wastes had not been invaded by the builder or by any civilising influences. But there are many good, honest, hard-working men among them. One, who for many years has supplied me with a regular yearly 'four dozen birch and two dozen heath,' I am sorry to know is now past work.

The birch spray is not used fresh. It is put aside to dry and toughen for some months. Then they 'break birch for brooms.' A faggot is opened, and the spray is broken by hand to the right size and laid in bundles. Breaking birch is often women's work. The 'bonds' that fasten the spray on to the handle are of hazel or withy, split and shaved with the knife into thick ribbons. They are soaked in water to make

The Heath Broom

them lissom. There is usually a little pool of water near the broom-maker's shed, where the bonds are soaked.

The broom-squarer gathers up the spray round the end of the stick, sitting in front of a heavy fixed block to which the further end of a bond is made fast. He pushes the near end of the bond into the butts of the spray, nearly at a right angle to the binding. He then binds by rolling the broom away from him, pulling it tight as it goes. When he has wound up to the length of the bond, the end is released and pushed into the work. Heath brooms have two bonds; birch, which are much longer, have three. A hole is bored between the strands of spray and through the stick, and a peg is driven tightly through, so that the spray cannot slip off the stick. The rough butts are then trimmed off, and the broom is complete.

They generally work in thatched sheds, the thatch commonly of heather. In old days it was usual to keep their money in some hole in the thatch inside; they considered it safer than keeping it in the cottages. The man would put up his hand into a place something like a bird's nest, and there was the money. An old friend, who knew their ways well, told me he had known of a sum of between three and four hundred pounds being kept in this way.

Another home industry was the rush-bottoming of chairs, and the making of workmen's dinner-baskets, mattings, and hassocks of the same rush. In old days this was much more frequent in the neighbourhood than now.

Many found work at home on winter evenings in making oak tile-pins, working by the firelight. But this industry has long been dead, tiles being now hung with pins of cast-iron.

CHAPTER VIII

VARIOUS ARTICLES FOUND IN COTTAGES

THOUGH not originally belonging to the buildings they were found in, many articles of furniture or ornament, that had been in houses of a better class, had found their way into cottages, and had remained there for generations.

Any one who has attended sales at cottages and farmhouses within the last thirty years must have seen many such things pass through the auctioneer's hands.

In the case of pieces of furniture they are necessarily in bad order, but were so excellently made in the beginning, that, as to their main structure, they have withstood all the hard wear and tear and ill treatment they have had to endure, and, after careful restoration, are good to live another two centuries. For instance, it is hard on a fine old dining-room chair of the time of the Commonwealth to have the weekly wash done in a large red-ware pan, standing on a bit of board laid across its empty seat; but such was the intermediate experience which had befallen the one shown. If chairs can feel, it must be glad to be restored to its ancient use, and to have its seat and back renewed in strong cow-hide, matching, as nearly as might be, the ragged piece of leather, that, seamed and torn and scarred, still remained fixed to the back by its time-blackened, broadheaded brass nails.

What had been the treatment of the mahogany chairs I cannot say, but the front rail of the one without arms shows

Oak Chair—Date about 1660   Mahogany Chair

Two Mahogany Armchairs

LIGHT BEDROOM CHAIRS

LACQUER LOOKING-GLASS

a good deal of wear from the grinding of hob-nailed boots, and was very loose in the joints when it came into my hands. I should judge that this chair was made in quite the early days of the use of mahogany.

The two mahogany armchairs have borne their trials bravely, and, after passing through the hands of a carpenter and a polisher, are as good as ever.

The two light chairs, with frames turned and painted in imitation of bamboo, are examples of patterns in general use in bedrooms early in the nineteenth century. Admirable chairs they are; light and strong and well-looking. It is a great pity that they are no longer made.

The lacquer looking-glass must have been a capital piece in its day; even now, though dinted and abraded, it is a cherished possession. Had it passed through the hands of a clever restorer it would have appeared to be as good as ever; in some ways even better; for old lacquer acquires a beautiful tone with age, rich and deep, and delightfully harmonious.

The lacquer tray, with shaped edge, is of the good old *papier-maché*. The ground is black; the ornament a free arabesque, some of whose main spaces are coloured green and chocolate; the whole is enriched with delicate gold pencillings. The tray was not rightly placed in the photograph. What shows as the left-hand side should have been the bottom, as the inner fringe of the pencilled ornament, which has much of the character of the lesser decorations of the rococo style, all droops downward. Its date, judging by the ornament, would be about 1760.

FOUND IN COTTAGES

The plain round mahogany tray is a nice example of one of the simple uses to which this wood was put at about the same date. The light has caught the grain in the photograph and makes it look rougher than it is. In reality it has a good surface that responds well to careful polishing, and is an admirable ground to its burden of silver and china tea-things. For, after its many years of cottage life, where, to judge by

LACQUER AND MAHOGANY TRAYS

its good condition, it must have stood unused upon some safe shelf, it is restored to use in a house of a better class.

It is a great pity that a very pretty kind of tea-tray of black *papier-maché*, with a decoration of roses and other flowers, partly of mother-o'-pearl and partly painted, evidently the simpler descendant of these older trays, and formerly in frequent use in humble and middle-class dwellings, should have gone out of make and use.

Odds and ends of pretty china and glass had also drifted

somehow into the cottages. Porcelain, generally cracked, but whole in the pieces shown, and a variety of pretty wine-glasses, I have found from time to time. The old liqueur glass is engraved with flowers, the taller ones with barley and vine-leaves.

Separate pieces and occasionally sets of pewter table ware, though oftener found in houses of a better class, come to light from time to time at farm sales, and sometimes single plates at cottages. The oldest and always the best-looking, in the case of plates and dishes, have the edge quite flat and rather wide.

Pewter mugs are still in use in public-houses. Of those in the picture the three to the left in the row of six are the oldest; No. 3, a mug without a handle, being of unusually good material. It must contain a larger proportion of silver than usual.

Many and various are the things that see the light at the sales at humble dwellings. Everything is routed out. Tall cupboards in farmhouses, that have not been cleared out for many years, disgorge the old swallowings of their topmost shelves. Even the owners do not know how the things came there.

Hour-Glass

Sometimes it is a prize—not to them—but to the collector—such as the old hour-glass, dating from the far-back time when clocks were scarce. Such hour-glasses were used in churches to remind the preacher—sermons were hour-long in those days—that even his discourse must have an end. But no doubt they were also used in kitchens, to time the roasting of a joint or the baking of bread.

ORIENTAL AND ENGLISH PORCELAIN AND GLASS

PEWTER TABLE WARE

PEWTER MUGS

The very old stone mortar came from a heap of rubbish outside some farm buildings. A smaller mortar of more modern shape is shown for comparison.

The cast-iron mortar is also very ancient. The bright brass

New and Old Stone Mortars

one is later. These brass mortars are so indestructible that they are still fairly plentiful. Every apothecary had one in the eighteenth century for the grinding and pounding of drugs. The iron one looks as if it might date

Iron and Brass Apothecaries' Mortars

from the fifteenth century. It has had a hole through the bottom, which has been rather clumsily patched with a thick pad of reddish brass, so that it rocks upon its base.

FOUND IN COTTAGES

The pretty pair of candlesticks must have been originally in a good house. When I bought them at a cottage sale for eighteen-pence (the lot including other articles) it was plain to see that they had had some hard wear in their day. The plating was nearly all gone, and the surface was dirty copper; but after passing through the silversmith's hands they came

PAIR OF PLATED CANDLESTICKS

out as nice a pair as one would wish to see, though less ornate than many of their time.

Among the many articles of diverse origin that have drifted into cottages and that have come to light at sales, or by the spontaneous offer on the part of the cottager of a thing that was to him useless and might bring in a shilling or two, is a group of objects relating to defence and protection. A special constable's staff of some heavy, close-grained wood is handsomely painted with the Royal Arms on a red ground that covers all but the handle. From the presence of the White Horse of Hanover, borne on the middle base of an inescutcheon, its date would be from

Special Constable's Staff Swinging Bludgeon

Wooden Rattle

1820 to 1831, when Acts were passed relating to the enrolment of special constables and the issue of these staves.

The heavy bludgeon, with a swinging, loaded head, was probably a weapon for domestic protection. It is capable

Leg Irons

of giving a terrible blow that would easily break a limb or crash into skull or ribs.

The rattle was to sound an alarm to attract the night-watchman. It is swung round and round, the momentum forcing the two wooden tongues to pass over the toothed

Small Iron Box, Four Inches Square

wheels. The noise, to the person using it, is an ear-piercing, screeching clatter. Later, it was used for scaring birds in fields of newly-sown grain.

The leg-irons were taken by what in former days answered to our present police, when they had reason to think that a prisoner was likely to be troublesome.

I know nothing of the history or origin of the little iron

180 OLD WEST SURREY

box, except that it was found, while gravel was being dug on Farley Heath, between Albury and Wonersh, within an area where relics of the Roman occupation have been discovered.

But few remain throughout the country of the old wooden stocks; but an example still exists at Shalford; where this old implement of punishment stands close to the churchyard wall.

The Stocks, Shalford

CHAPTER IX

TOOLS AND RURAL INDUSTRIES

THE greater number of the hand-tools in use in country places have gone on, without appreciable change of form or method of using, for hundreds of years. These tools have come by their forms simply from necessity, and when they have arrived at what is most convenient for an unchanging kind of use, there they remain. The form and size and weight have become fixed for certain classes of work. There may be slight local distinctions, and the tool may be in two or three sizes, but that is all.

It is only when whole ranges of conditions of life change, and certain industries cannot be carried on in the old ways, that the tools must alter to fit the newer needs.

Nearly the whole of the change from hand labour to machine work in agriculture has taken place within my recollection. In the old days hay was mown with the scythe, and made with the fork and rake. All the tools wanted hung in a small space in the labourer's back-kitchen or outhouse. Sometimes there was a large three-pronged wooden fork—a tool of great antiquity, but later used only for barley; and the farmer had a wide drag-rake with iron teeth. But for the actual needs of hay-making there were but three tools—scythe, fork, and wooden rake.

Now, to be fully equipped for hay-making, there are a number of horse implements, the larger ones requiring a pair of horses. First, there is the mower, then a choice of varieties of horse-drawn machines for throwing up and turning the hay—kickers, tedders, swathe-turners, and finally the horse-rake. The rakes are of fairly simple construction, but the other implements are of complicated mechanism, and all of them require housing, repairing, painting, and lubricating. The old hand-tools might all be hung upon one nail or peg; the modern horse machines must have a considerable range of

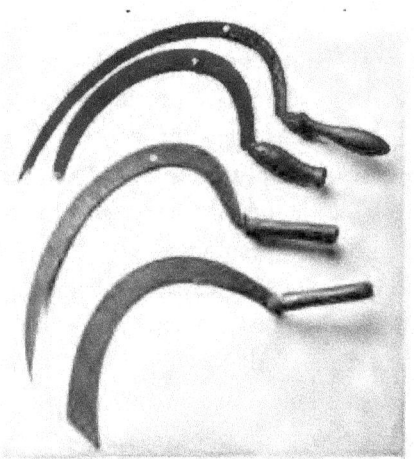

REAPING-HOOKS AND FAG-HOOK

shedding. And all these cumbersome things, involving so much housing and care, are for use within perhaps four weeks of the year!

One of the few changes in the form and use of hand-tools that has occurred within my recollection has been in those used for the reaping of corn. Before my time, but well into the early half of the last century, wheat was reaped with the sickle. It was shaped like the reaping-hook, but had a finely-toothed edge. The under-side of the blade towards the edge was ridged transversely, much like a toothing-plane, so that the edge was a saw. When I was a biggish child, strong and delighting in any bodily exercise, I sometimes had a day in the harvest-field. My reaping-hook—rip-hook it was always called—is the third from the top in the picture; the two above it are older ones that have seen more wear.

Anyone who has never done a day's work in the harvest-field would scarcely believe what dirty work it is. Honest sweat and dry dust combine into a mixture not unlike mud. Hay-making is drawing-room work in comparison.

Nowadays, when wheat is not cut with a machine, it is 'fagged' with the fag-hook, the lowest tool in the picture. It is a much heavier tool, and the way of using it is quite different; 'ripping' and 'fagging' are quite distinct. The fag-hook has a square crook or step, just after it leaves the handle, bringing the blade into a lower plane than the hand. This is to protect the hand in slashing through brambles and rough stuff in hedge-trimming and to save the knuckles from being skinned against stumps. The blade of the reaping-hook goes straight out of the handle.

In reaping, the left hand grasps a handful of the standing corn and the tool cuts it with a sharp, dragging action. In fagging, the left hand holds a light stick or a small handful of stiff-strawed corn, and with it bends back the stems to be cut. The tool is used with a slashing action. The work is quicker and easier.

I have lately asked several farmers and work-people why corn was ever cut by the slower and more laborious process of reaping, for the fag-hook is no new tool. It was always in use for trimming hedges and cutting rough grass in odd places. No one has given me a satisfactory answer. Trying to think what the reason may have been—for I know that the old-time farmers were shrewd folk, not given to wasting labour even when it was much more plentiful—I can only come to the conclusion that the slower and more careful method allowed the corn to stand and ripen a few days longer before being cut, and that with the rougher methods of the fag-hook it has to be cut a little greener.

Fagging cuts closer, leaving less stubble, but there is no gain in the end. 'It isn't picked up so close.' Some of the older people say that in fagging a 'man leaves his wages on the ground.'

In the older days of reaping, when every straw on the field was taken in the hand, it was a good day's work for a man to reap an acre, though I have also heard of a woman reaping an acre; even in this neighbourhood, where the acre is reckoned at 'eight score,' that is to say, 160 rods. Down in Sussex, Chichester way, they reckon it at only 'six score,' equal to 120 rods.

This old abuse of different measures, and also of various measures of capacity, within districts by no means distant from each other, still largely exists. It seems almost incredible that there should not be standard measures of capacity throughout the country, but so it is; for instance, there is or was the Winchester bushel, of a different capacity to the ordinary bushel, and so on.

The distinction of 'strike measure' and 'heaped measure' is of course reasonable, whatever the standard may be; 'strike measure,' level with the lip of the bushel, being used for grain, or peas, or anything that will lie close, and heaped measure for potatoes, or apples, or anything of a size or shape that leaves cavities between.

TOOLS AND RURAL INDUSTRIES 185

In the old days wheat was often dibbled. A labourer with a pair of dibbling-irons walked backwards across the field, dibbling two lines of holes. Two children, six or seven years old, followed him, dropping a grain or two into each hole. It was said that dibbled wheat grew finer than any other. Peas and beans were sometimes sown in the same way. These irons are a little shorter than walking-sticks; their bluntly-pointed ends can be thrust into the ground at a fair pace, the two hands working alternately.

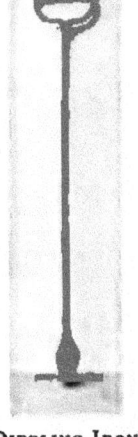

DIBBLING-IRON

The old wooden plough is seldom seen now, though it lingers on one good old farm within reach, and is well liked by the men who work it. It is generally used with two coulters, though only one was in place when this picture was done. A forked stick lies along the left-hand stilt, the forked end resting in an iron loop on the inside of the thick end of the beam. It is for the ploughman to reach and hook away, without stopping his team, any roots or tough weedy rubbish that hangs up between the share and coulters.

I can remember when corn was commonly threshed with the flail. The old people about here always called it *frail*. It is interesting to examine the simple old tool and see how it was made. The picture shows a little more than half its length. The right-hand part is the handle; the left, the swingel (soft 'g' as in angel). The head of the handle has an iron pin with a flat head. The pin passes down into the handle, and is riveted in place through its neat iron ferrule. It is a rather dainty piece of blacksmith's work. All the rest was made on the farm, of ash and raw hide.

2 A

The loop of the handle-head is made of a bit of tough green ash, whittled into shape. Its square shoulders fit loosely under the head of the pin, and a channel is hollowed on each side for the shaft of the pin, so that it can revolve freely. The thicker butts of the bent ash loop are securely

WOODEN PLOUGH

bound with waxed twine, and one half of the flail is complete.

The swingel is a thicker rod, about the same length as the handle, viz. 41 inches. The end where it joins the head has a depression whittled out of it an inch from the tip. A stout raw-hide loop is passed over this, and is fixed with a binding of a thinner strip of the same. Another loop of raw hide makes a link connecting the other two. The word 'flail' is a highly respectable descendant of *flagellum*.

TOOLS AND RURAL INDUSTRIES 187

The threshing of corn on the barn floor was one of the happiest of country sights and sounds. From after harvest to the spring of the next year, stored in the ample bays of the barn, it could be threshed out as it was wanted, hand-winnowed, and put away in the granary.

The granaries themselves of the older fashion are beautiful buildings. I am thankful that on many farms they are still standing, though buildings so perfectly in harmony

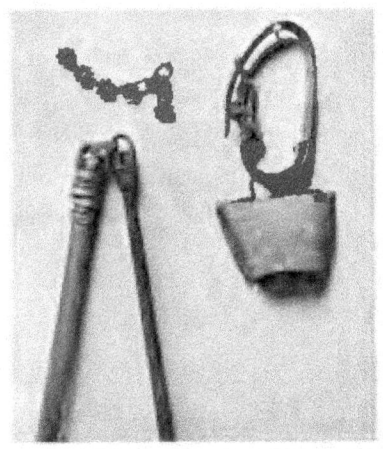

FLAIL, CURB-CHAIN, AND LARGE SHEEP-BELL

with the sentiment of rural English life are now rarely erected. They are usually over a waggon-shed, carried upon short piers with rat-proof caps of stone or oak. Rough stone steps lead up to the granary door and add much to the pictorial value of the building. One of them is shown at p. 36.

Indeed, in these sad days of cheap building, and corrugated iron roofing, and machinery, one looks in vain for many of the lost beauties of country life. Women, gleaning in the harvest-field—'leasing' as they used to call it—are now no longer seen. The pitiless, grasping iron contrivances pick up the stray ears too closely. The mower carrying his scythe is to be remembered only, for he is rarely to be met.

In the older days the wives and children of farm-servants were allowed to glean or 'lease' on the fields of the farm where the father was employed, before the sheaves were carried. If others came who were not entitled to the

A MOWER

privilege, they were roped off the field, where it was free of sheaves, by a rope stretched between two horses, and so carried down the field. After the corn was carried, most farmers allowed anybody to glean. The children held the ears on long stalks, in their hands close up to the heads, making neat bundles. The ears on short stems were dropped into an apron pocket.

The corn so gleaned, after being threshed, was ground at

the mill free of charge and sent home to the cottages. In a good season the gleaners could usually get enough to last well through the winter.

Those cheerful gangs of hay-makers and harvesters—are they gone for ever? Let us hope not. What happy and well-earned meals those were that were eaten sitting under the shady side of the hedge bank, where an oak gave wide overhead shelter.

The mower's meals were many and his wholesome drink was much, but he toiled the long day through with all the strength of his body—every muscle in full play.

Often they began work at daylight, and on some farms it was the custom that the man who came first got a pint of ale.

The mowers' regular meals were: breakfast at six, lunch at half-past nine, dinner at noon, afternoon lunch at four, supper at seven, when the farmer generally gave each man a bottle of beer or cider.

A man would mow an acre of hay a day for half-a-crown or three shillings, but he could mow an acre and a half of barley. A first-rate man has mown two acres of barley. Now, an acre of hay cannot be hand-mown under ten shillings.

The drink—beer or cider—was carried in the wooden harvest-bottle—a little barrel strongly hooped with iron. The largest are about ten inches high, and will hold a gallon. Like all good barrels they are of oak, with a projecting mouth-piece, and just above it a hole for the vent-peg. The vent-peg and cork are tied to the rope-handle, so that they cannot go astray; two holes are bored in the base of the mouth-block, through which a cord or leather thong is passed, to carry by.

I have some two dozen of them of all sizes; some quite tiny, of a half-pint capacity, evidently made for children. Some have been painted, the paint being nearly always of a good quality of blue; though the large one in the illustration has been painted white, with black hoops—but this was one of a set that had belonged to a squire.

A harvest bottle, when not too large or heavy, is a pleasant thing to drink from, and when a fine labouring man drinks

HARVEST BOTTLES

standing, with his head thrown back and his two arms raised, the attitude is generally a strong and graceful one.

The head of the little barrel is always made of one piece. In one that I have, the head has split, and has evidently leaked, and the leak has been stopped with pitch.

The owner's initials were usually branded on both heads; some of those I have show three ownerships, bearing three sets of initials.

One large bottle shows P. R. in a very old kind of lettering. Branded right across this is F. F. S. and above and below this, C. F. The F. F. S. is the most recent; one can tell by the style of the letter. Moreover, our sensible ancestors were content with one Christian name, and, indeed, what can any Christian want with more! F. B. and H. H. were modest drinkers; three half-pints of liquor is as much as their bottles will hold.

On a Harvest Bottle

A W could manage his half-gallon. His mark is a very old one, and the lettering is so pretty that I thought it deserved a picture to itself.

The letters are incised, not branded. His bottle bears a much more recent A. C. C.

T. H. made a modest little mark of some antiquity.

W. K.—this mark is not done with a regular brand, but freehand with a hot iron. The man who made it got the twist the wrong way in the right-hand part of the K. This bottle bears another mark, I. M., also of old character. Another, a three-quart size, has the head almost covered with records of ownership. R. M. and I. M. are branded, P. B. is incised. It has had pitch run into the joint where the head fits the staves.

Lettering on a Harvest Bottle

R. S.'s bottle was made of a very beautiful piece of oak. Another H. H. took a dark blue quart to the field. E. B. used a bottle hooped with wicker. These are still made; I use one for taking out the water to boil for picnic tea.

Some of the older harvest bottles have the carrying-cord made of horse-hair, generally black and white; sometimes black, white, and chestnut. Generally it is in a close, tight plait of three, but in one I have it is a kind of square plait of four strands, something like the working of a whip-thong. When these horse-hair cords were used the maker was not content with passing the ends through the holes and putting a knot in the end of the cord, but they were stopped with neat wooden plugs driven tight into the holes by the side of the cord.

When the harvest bottles were large and too heavy to drink from in comfort, a mug was used, often a horn one. No doubt these horns were the ordinary drinking vessels of the old-time labouring folk. They may still be had, and a thin-lipped horn is a favourite beer-mug with some old-

HORN MUGS

fashioned people, though their general use has long gone out in favour of glasses.

The horn mug is a section of bullock's horn, cleansed, scraped, and polished, and pared away inside at the top to make a fine-edged lip. A groove was cut all round inside, about a quarter of an inch from the bottom, and a flat disk of horn was fitted tightly to the opening just below it. The edge of the disk was pared to fit into the groove, softened by heat, and then partly forced and partly sprung into its place, making a perfectly water-tight joint.

The largest of the mugs shown must have been cut from a horn of unusual size. It is nearly four inches across, and stands four and a half inches high. The ordinary size is

TOOLS AND RURAL INDUSTRIES

three and a half to four inches high, and less than three inches across the top. The horn next to it has an ornament that looks as if it had been done by a series of impressions

LEATHER BOTTLES—THE LARGEST 8 INCHES LONG

of an iron die or punch over a sheet of tin-foil; a little of the silvery foil being stamped into the surface at each stroke.

The old leather bottle of Tudor and Jacobean days, and

LEATHER BOTTLE, CUT TO HOLD CART-GREASE

who knows how long before, has long been out of use. With the exception of the ends, that answer to the heads of the oak harvest-bottles, they were made of one piece of leather.

The leather was no doubt moulded wet on a wooden form, which must have been in three pieces like a boot-tree—the upper piece to define the shape of the shoulders and neck, and the middle one to slip out first to liberate the others before the ends were sewn in. As they went out of use they were very commonly used with an opening cut in one side, to hang up in farm stables to hold cart-grease. The fact of

THE SAW-PIT

their having been saturated with the mixture of grease and wood-tar no doubt accounts for the survival of many of them in fairly sound condition.

Now, when every builder has his steam-saw, the old country saw-pits have gone out of use. But in the older days it was good to see and hear the rhythmical working of the great pit-saw, and to note the clever, handy way the men would shift the mighty tree-trunks with lever and rollers. And the saw-pit was generally in some pretty place

The Cider-Mill

The Cider-Press

close to sharply-sloping ground, so that the bottom of it was kept dry by natural drainage. And it was easy to see how the word 'top-sawyer' came to have a special significance in country speech, in the way of meaning something rather grand, or, at any rate, a good bit raised above something or somebody else.

Cider is still made with the old wooden press. The apples are first crushed by a roller in the cider-mill. Two men work it together by a handle on each side, while one of them presses the stream of apples down towards the roller. The crushed pulp falls into a tub, and is then put into coarse fibre bags. These are then packed one over the other in the press with boards between. The picture shows how the heavy presser is screwed down on to the bags of pulp till they are quite flattened, and all the juice that can be squeezed out of them has come away.

The heaps of apples, mostly of the poorest of the orchard produce, do not look at all inviting. Many are muddy and bruised, but in they go, mud and all; and when a mug of the freshly-pressed juice is offered, and is accepted with some internal hesitation, whose outward expression is repressed for civility's sake, one is pleasantly surprised to find what a delicious drink, tasting clean and pure and refreshing, is this newly-drawn juice of quite second and third-rate apples. For though cider of a kind is frequently made, it is by no means a cider country, and no refinements, either of growing or making, are practised.

Copse-cutting is one of the handy labourer's winter harvests, and is done by piecework. One of the industries that grow out of it, namely hoop-making, was described at some length in 'Wood and Garden.' It is the making of

Copse-Cutter Faggoting Up

hoops for barrels and packing-cases; hoops shaved on both sides and made up in neat bundles of standard lengths. The shavings make a capital and durable thatch. Hoop-making, which is still carried on in the woods of the district on a rather large scale, is probably not an ancient industry. It must have grown with the modern facilities for communi-

THE HURDLE-MAKER

cation, for the largest and longest of the hoops go to the tropics for sugar hogsheads.

But another industry that goes on in the copses in winter and spring is probably much older and is still well alive. This is the making of wattle hurdles for sheepfolds. They are made of hazel, ash, or willow.

The hurdle-maker has a long-shaped block, slightly curved, called the hurdle frame, something over six feet in length, with vertical holes to hold the uprights that form, as it were, the warp of the hurdle. These are round rods, pointed at the bottom; they are driven into the holes and stand upright. The man then weaves in horizontally the smaller split rods till he has filled up the hurdle. When he comes to either end he gives the rod a clever twist that opens the fibres and gives it something the character of a rope, so that it passes, tough-stranded and unbroken, round the end uprights. In the middle of the hurdle, about one-third down from the top, he leaves an open space. This is for the shepherd to slip his hand into, to carry two hurdles at a time, one under each arm; or he puts two or three together, passes a stake through the opening, and carries them on his back with the stake over his shoulder.

The hurdle-maker wears a stout leather pad on his left side to protect his clothing where the rub of the loose rods in weaving and splitting would otherwise tear them about. Some of the men use two tools, some only one. This is a form of hand-bill that acts as chopper, cleaving tool, mallet, and, held short by the back of the blade, as a knife to trim off projecting ends and give the work a general tidying up.

The old local word *rozzling, rostling,* or *rahstling* stands for an industry akin to hurdle-making, but coming within the work of the hedger. It is the making of a wattled fence on a hedge-bank. The hedger drives in stout stakes a few inches apart and weaves or rostles in his rods of hazel, ash, oak, or chestnut. Two thicker rods at the top, worked together and crossing between each stake, make a firm finish.

The shepherd's crook is a tool from the earliest ages. It is for catching a sheep by the hind leg. The one shown is of a fine old pattern. The next picture is of two sheep-bells of the usual kind, and a sheep-marking iron. It is dipped in Stockholm tar or colouring matter, to print upon the fleece. A very large old sheep-bell is shown at p. 187.

Every farm had its steel-yard, the usual appliance for weighing. It is an instrument of great antiquity, still used all over the East. It has two adjustments, one for heavy weights and one for lighter. The four-sided bar on which the bob hangs has two scales of graduation. In the case of the alternative adjustment, the steel-yard hangs the other way up, suspended by the hook that hangs between the weight (sack of potatoes in the picture) and the bob. The bar is so engraved that it shows on the upper of its two diagonal faces the graduation proper to the adjustment in use.

SHEPHERD'S CROOK

MARKING-IRON AND SHEEP BELLS

The country people call it the 'stilly'd,' with a heavy accent on the first syllable, and the second nearly suppressed.

TOOLS AND RURAL INDUSTRIES 201

An interesting local tool is a kind of spade used on the heathy wastes for cutting heath-turf for burning. It is used as shown (on page 203). The man throws the weight of his body against the heavy cross-handle. It looks a cumbersome, lumbering thing, but in actual use its weight helps

STEEL-YARD

the work. The cutting of heath-sods for fuel is one of the commoners' privileges.

Bricklayers are now so constantly moving about, often to far distant jobs, that there are not nearly so many of the old stay-at-home sort, who have that perfect knowledge of local ways, but here is one of them (p. 204). He is dead now, but for many years I had to do with him on garden and other building work. He was nearly stone deaf, left-handed, and had lost one eye, but his work was some of the truest and best I have ever seen. His whole heart was in it.

2 c

The timber-waggon, with its massive wheels and strong body, has changed but little. Its solidly-framed, horizontal transoms that carry the timber, rise a few inches above the top of the wheels; and, as will be seen by the picture, the

Tool for Cutting Heath-Turf

hind-wheels with their transom can be slid back along the pole to accommodate the length of timber to be loaded. The wheels are very broad, for it has to go into the soft ground of the woodlands, often through unmetalled lanes, or the deep sandy tracks of rough heathy places.

CUTTING HEATH-TURF

In the quite old days timber was loaded with a triangle of straight poles and a chain and pulley, but ever since I can remember by an easier method. The timber-waggon is drawn up by the side of the tree-trunk, which lies about as far from it as the edge of the roadway that shows in the picture. There are two chains, long and strong, called the rolling chains. These have one end attached to the timber-

THE OLD BRICKLAYER

carriage, while the other is carried under the log, brought up over it and passed right away over the middle of the waggon to the further side, where the horses are waiting. Stout pieces of oak lean from the log on the ground up to the end of each transom over the wheels, to form a rolling way. The hooks of the whippances that dangle below the horses' hocks are hooked into the free ends of the chains; the horses, answering the carter's word, strain forward to their work; the

TOOLS AND RURAL INDUSTRIES 205

log rolls up the inclined plane and comes to rest on the transoms.

Unless the trees are very large, two will lie side by side, and often a third on the top. There is a hole at each end of the transom in which a short iron can be fixed vertically to stop the tendency to roll outward when the load is of longer, thinner trees, such as larch, or spruce, or Scotch fir. The chains go round the whole load and are strained tight

Timber-Waggon

with bars. When loaded it will be seen that the two parts of the timber-carriage are fixed together, not by the pole, which is quite loose, but by the rigid load.

A lifetime of driving about in country places teaches one to drive very carefully in passing the tails of some loads. The long load of slender larches is one of these; the extreme end sways about in a way that it is well to beware of. So is also a builder's load of long ladders, and the jumping ends of flooring boards, burdens that also, if the pace is smart and the road uneven, and especially downhill, get into a way of swaying dangerously from side to side.

Another of these dangers, when it is getting dusk, is the bundle of rod and strap-iron that the country carriers bring out from the towns for the blacksmiths. It sticks out some feet from the back of their hooded vans, and though it is usual to tie a piece of sacking over the end, this wise pre-

AN OLD ROADSIDE LIMEKILN

caution and useful danger-signal is sometimes overlooked, and it is as well to be on the lookout.

Thatching, though almost extinct as a way of roofing cottages, is still a necessity for covering ricks. But the work for this temporary purpose cannot compare with that of the old roof thatcher, with his 'strood' or 'frail' to hold the loose straw, and his spars—split hazel rods pointed at each end—that with a dexterous twist in the middle make neat pegs for the fastening of the straw rope that he cleverly twists with a simple implement called a 'wimble.' The lowest course was finished with an ornamental double

THE ARCH OF MYSTERY

bordering of rods with a diagonal criss-cross pattern between, all neatly pegged and firmly held down by the spars.

The light, sandy farm land, of which there is so much in the neighbourhood, needs the addition of lime in some form or other. Root crops of the turnip and cabbage family suffer from 'finger-and-toe' or 'clubbing.' While the plant is in a young state the root thickens into a tough, shapeless mass and the top withers. The farmer and gardener know, when they see this, that the land must be limed. Farms throughout the district had their own kilns for burning the lime. The extensive property to which the grand old farm, whose barn is shown at p. 24, with many other farms, belonged, had several of these kilns. Wheat from this farm was carted to the Guildford market, a distance of seven miles, and the waggons brought back chalk from a pit on the same property near Guildford.

Many of these kilns have been destroyed, but a fair number remain. They were built in steeply-sloping ground by or near a roadside, where the loads of chalk could be drawn up to their top level. They are interesting wayside objects, and some of them that have been overgrown with brushwood, or that stand in what has become woodland, grown up during the sixty years or more that have passed since they were used, have an air of mystery that still brings back to me the thrills of fearful joy that they excited in my childish mind. One in particular, already thickly wooded, and only dimly showing its low, round-arched portal under the dark overgrowth of holly and bramble, I used to think was the entrance, through interminable underground passages, to some such castle of mystery as those that are described in Mrs. Radcliffe's romances.

The larger blocks of chalk were built up inside the kiln (which is circular in plan and open at the top), in the form of a rough arch, corresponding more or less to the opening, and the smaller pieces of chalk were filled in above. The space underneath was crammed with furze faggots, and a certain amount of burning converted the chalk into lime.

Every field on a farm has its name; as a rule every farm that had a limekiln, unless it had other rough land or adjoined a common, had its furze-field.

TOOLS AND RURAL INDUSTRIES 209

This name remains on such farms, though the field may have been put meanwhile to other uses; when it occurs, it is an indication that there is probably an old limekiln not far off.

A former industry, now almost extinct in this neighbourhood, was the catching of moles with the old wooden mole-trap.

The traps were home-made. The body of the thing is a piece of wood $5\frac{1}{4}$ by 3 inches wide and half-an-inch thick. In this, seven holes are bored with a half-inch bit, three across each end and one in the middle. Two pieces of green ash are whittled into shape to form the hoops. Their ends are split, passed up through the outer holes and wedged from the top; a small groove having been cut or scooped all along on their inner sides. The bark remains on the outsides of the hoops.

The picture shows the arrangement of the strings. The short, lower length of string has a plain knot at its end. It is passed down through the middle hole, and is fixed from below by a forked peg called the 'mumble-pin' or 'mumble-peg.' The butt of the peg has a rounded end, and goes a very little way into the hole, only just enough to jam the knotted end of the string and to remain in position while the trap is being set. It holds a little firmer when the longer upright length of string is fixed to the spring 'bender.' The two ends of string connected with the brass wires are loose when the trap is set, the wires being pressed into position in their grooves on the inner sides of the ash hoops. In the picture, for the sake of clearness, the wires are shown out of place.

The trap is set an inch or so below the ground, so that the space within the ash hoops corresponds to the mole's

2 D

run. To keep it down against the upward pull of the 'bender' two sticks are passed diagonally across it; they are thrust firmly into the ground, nipping down the top edges of the trap. Only one of these is shown in the picture; the other crosses it, passing into the ground the opposite way.

The mumble-pin is set so fine that the least touch of the

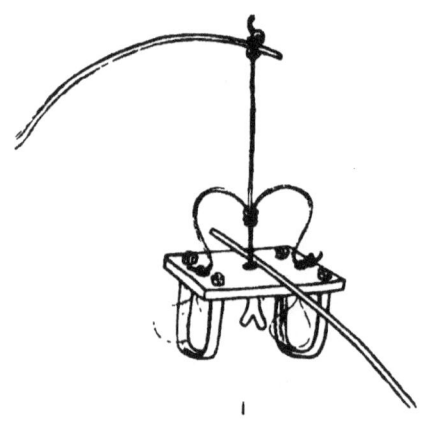

WOODEN MOLE-TRAP

mole's snout throws it out, releasing the string. The bender, with its strong spring, pulls up the string, carrying with it the two side ones with their wires, in one or other of which the mole is caught.

As traps go it is a merciful one, for it is known that a very slight shock kills a mole, and it is very rarely that a trapped one is not found dead.

CHAPTER X

THE CARTER'S PRIDE

In the older days the country towns on market days were gay with the brightly-painted farm-waggons with their well-groomed teams.

There was an amicable rivalry among the carters as to the dressing of their horses, for the brightly-polished brass ornaments and the gay rosettes of worsted ribbon were the carter's own property, and when not on the horses were often arranged as a trophy over the cottage fireplace. Foremost among these ornaments were the ear-bells, with their upright plume of black and white, or red and yellow horsehair, that followed the top strap of the headstall and buckled in just above the blinkers. Sometimes in the place of the plume there was the ornament of three tinkling bells, or the circular brass plate, hinged at the top, that flashed as it swung, often turning right over as Dobbin tossed his head; and there was a brass plate with shaped edge, engraved with a horse and cart or some other device, that went upon the nose-band. Then there were the 'face-pieces,' in a great variety of pattern; also used below the collar, three or four one above another. Those of a raised crescent shape are of an extremely ancient design; the lowest one on the right, with three crescents joined, I think I remember to be identical with an Assyrian horse-ornament. Other portions of the harness were profusely ornamented with small round brass studs and heart-shaped and bossy brasses.

THE CARTER'S TROPHY OF HORSE ORNAMENTS

SMALL BELLS AND SWINGING BRASSES

THE CARTER'S PRIDE

The love of decorating his horses is still a matter of pleasant pride to the good carter, and when I see a well-looking team, made unusually smart for the road or town, I know that the carter is a good fellow, who takes a right pride in his work and cattle.

But the number of the pretty teams are few compared to those of the older days, when one still heard the pleasant music of the 'latten' bells. A few years ago I bought two sets of these at a farm sale. An old carter standing by said to me, 'I mind when we always went to market with

LATTEN BELLS

the teams dressed and the latten bells on, and when they wore *they*, the horses was just as proud as the carters was.' Latten is an old English word for a kind of brass or bronze, answering to the French *laiton*.

There were four rings of bells in the set, and each set had four bells, except the one with three of the largest bells of deep tone; each set made its own chord, while the whole clanged and jingled in pleasant harmonies.

The leather hood, plain in the one shown, was often scalloped or evenly jagged at the lower edge, and generally had a pretty running ornament of barley, incised with a small gouge in the surface of the leather. A red woollen fringe hung inside the hood all round; sometimes it came only a little way down, but generally was so long as to hide the bells completely. The two spikes passed down the two sides of the collar along the hames.

The original use of bells on the harness was to give notice in the narrow lanes, so that a carter hearing a distant team, could either wait before entering the lane, or draw to the side in good time at some wider part.

There is a legend of two carters who purposely ignored the warning, met in the middle of a narrow lane, and fought the matter out. How the battle ended and how the teams and waggons were got out remains unrecorded in local history.

Ear-caps were prettily braided in gay colours, edged with brightly-coloured tufts, and tied in place with worsted ribbon to match. Manes were plaited and tied with ribbons also matching; and then Prince and Smiler, Dragon and Champion; or Diamond, Violet, Punch and Jolly, as the case might be, tossing their heads to make their pretty music, and pawing the ground to show their eagerness, went proudly on their townward way.

EAR-CAPS

Some of the older harness was needlessly heavy, but it seems a pity that the great upstanding flaps that stood up above the collar, that looked so handsome and were such a comforting protection to the horse's withers when turned down in wet weather, should now be so little used.

THE CARTER'S PRIDE 215

The illustration shows a heavy old bridle, with the head-stall, all but the straps, cut out of one piece of leather.

AN OLD FARM BRIDLE

In old days horse-shoes seem to have been of a very wide shape, such as would now be made for horses with

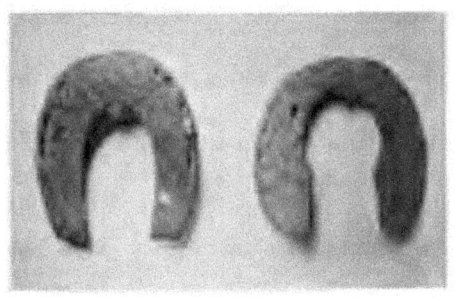

OLD HORSE-SHOES

corns; but I have seen this old pattern so often that I take it to have been in general use. These were found when a hedge was grubbed down on my own ground.

In the old days bullock-teams were used for ploughing and other farm work, as they are to this day in parts of Sussex. Sometimes an old bullock-shoe is turned up in ploughing. They are like half horse-shoes, divided to suit

PLOUGHMAN BRINGING HOME THE HORSES

the divided hoof, and widened to the back like the right-hand horse-shoe in the picture.

I have often wondered what may have been the origin of some of the curious words, or rather sounds, by which the carter communicates with his horses. 'Woh' for 'stop' is familiar to us all. For going forward the word of command is 'pull up'; this is intelligible, though the words as uttered can hardly be recognised, but the alternatives 'Gee-whee' or 'Gee-whut-ah,' or the still more

THE CARTER'S PRIDE

mysterious 'mither-wee' ('come to me' or 'turn round'), seem to be outside the bounds of either etymology or syntax. And these curious words are not exactly pronounced; they are produced with a rumbling, cavernous-sonorous kind of inarticulation, as if they passed through

THE EVENING DRINK

an open throat from the depths of the stomach. Then in 'Gee-whut-ah' the first syllable is about two tones higher than the rest. In 'mither-wee' the second syllable of 'mither' jumps up an octave and comes down again upon the 'wee'; and the whole intonation is so much muffled and broadened that it sounds as if the vowels were 'o' and 'u' instead of 'i' and 'e'. There is also a suspicion of the jodelling trick about it. But it is one of the true old country sounds, and long may it remain in use.

CHAPTER XI

OLD COUNTRY FOLK—THEIR WAYS OF SPEECH

It is sad to think that, within a few years, death will have claimed the few yet living of the old people who retain the speech and manner of the earlier part of the nineteenth century. Born and brought up in remote and quiet country villages and hamlets, many of them can neither read nor write, and I have met with some who have never been ten miles away from their birthplace. But they are by no means among the dull ones of the earth; indeed, their simple wisdom and shrewdness are in many ways quite equal to those of their brethren in the wider world.

Their lives have been perhaps all the happier in that they have been concerned with few wants and few responsibilities; and if their thoughts are mainly of hay-time and harvest, and root-crops, and the care of sheep and cattle, shall we presume to think that these interests are of less account than our own; for, after all, what can be of greater need or of more supreme importance?

They are good to have to do with, these kindly old people. Bright and cheerful of face, pleasant and ready of speech, courteous of manner, they are a precious remnant of those older days when men's lives were simpler and quieter; free from the stress and strain and restless movement, and endless hurry and struggle against time, and from all the petty worrying distractions that fret the daily life of the more modern worker. So pleasantly does this make itself felt that to be with one of these old people for an hour's quiet chat is a distinctly restful and soothing experience.

It is good to hear their ideas of life, and their stories of actual experience, told in the homely wording of their limited vocabulary, and there is a charm in the cheery old

An Old Labourer

country voice, with its whimsical twists of quavering modulation. And no less pleasant is the old country manner, whose ready courtesy expresses kindly welcome and cordial good fellowship.

Among these old folks one hears with pleasure many a terse old phrase and local saying, and many a word of good old English, that those who have the pretension of knowing better have somehow lost, either by sheer neglect, or by letting some rank weed of a word grow up and choke and kill, and usurp the place of one so much older and better. For instance, the fine old verb 'to abide' is still in their mouths. 'Bide still' says the cottage grandmother to a restless child, or 'I'll bide at home till the rain gives over.'

'Stand on a cheer, Gooerge, ye'll have moor might,' said an old father, when his son was trying to pull a nail out of a beam at arm's length. 'Might' in this sense is nearly lost to us; the only hold we seem to keep of it, except in the adjective and adverb forms, is in the idioms, 'with all his might' and 'with might and main.' Why have we become so shy of the good old words? I hear the old carpenter say of the new gate-post, 'Rare (rear) it up,' and of the tree-trunk 'Saw it asunder,' whereas I suppose we should say 'Stand it up on end,' or 'Stand it upright' and 'Saw it in two' or 'Saw it across,' surely all weaker and more cumbersome ways of saying the same thing.

Some words they use in a sense different to that usually accepted. If a child has done wrong and the father says he will 'chastise' him, it does not mean that he will corporally punish, but that he will exhort him, or 'give him a good talking to.' When, in summer, horses and cattle are worried by flies, they say the flies 'tarrify' them. 'To remember' is 'to mind'; 'I mind the time when such a thing happened.' To use abusive language to a person is to 'scandalise.' This is quite good old English, though generally obsolete. When a small child shows precocious intelligence and a desire to assert itself, the proud mother, or her admiring visitor, says, 'He's a little masterpiece.' The old woman 'grafts' her gown when she puts in a patch, and gleaning is known as 'leasing.' Tendons, or any visible cord-like muscles, as on the back of the hand, are always called 'leaders.'

There are certain stock phrases that are sure to be used when the occasion comes. A sick person, who falls away into a state of emaciation, is described as 'Nothing but a frame.' An old husband or wife dies, and the remaining one always says, 'I've lost my best friend.' When they were married they just as surely said, 'I've got a good partner.' How far the use of these words and phrases extends beyond one district I am unable to say. I speak of my recollection of what I have heard in my own corner of West Surrey—that which is nearest to Sussex and Hampshire.

There are a number of old local names of birds and small wild animals, &c., some of which are still in use. Thus, the green woodpecker is a 'yaffles,' the wagtail a 'dish-washer'; the wren a 'puggy' or 'juggy-wren'; the night-jar is called 'puckridge' or 'eve-jar'; the swift, 'squeaker'; the whitethroat, 'nettle-creeper' or 'hay-builder'; the red-backed shrike, 'butcher-bird' or 'bee-eater'; the common heron, 'Jack-heron,' and the wryneck, 'rining-bird.' This bird comes at the time when the oak-bark is stripped. 'When we hears that we very soon thinks about rining the oaks.' 'Rine' (rind) is the usual equivalent of bark.

The dormouse is called 'sleeper' or 'sleep-mouse'; the long-tailed field-mouse 'bean-eater'; the field-vole and bank-vole 'sheep-dog mouse.'

The large stag-beetles are 'pincher-bobs,' cock-chafers are 'may-bees,' the large dragon-flies are 'adder-spears.'

The rabbits' burrow is always a 'bury.' Young geese are 'gulls,' never goslings.

'Agen' is an interesting old word. 'Agen the ge-at' (both g's hard) does not mean 'against the gate,' but 'near the gate.' It seems to have the same sense as the 'over against' of the Bible.

Our old countrymen add one more to the many ways of sounding 'ough,' for they say the pig eats out of a 'tro'; this is so familiar that I find myself saying 'pig-tro' quite unconsciously.

The use of the word 'dirt,' in the sense of earth or soil, is interesting and not easy to define. As far as I am able to observe, it means any surface earth that is being moved or has lately been moved, or is likely to be disturbed or taken away. The hedger mends hollows in a bank after 'gapping' and 'plashing' by 'chucking up some dirt' as he scours the ditch. Extra soil that is thrown out in excavating for a building, or that is moved for levelling, is so many loads of 'dirt,' unless it is sand or clay, when it is called by those names. Yet in describing the soil of a garden he would not say there is a foot and a half of good 'dirt'; he would call it 'mould.' He is speaking of it in a state of repose, although garden ground is always liable to be disturbed. But in planting an apple-tree he would lay out the roots in the hole and sprinkle a little 'dirt' carefully over them before filling in.

In this use the word 'dirt' is not a term of contempt, nor does it bear any sense of uncleanliness, though this naturally grows out of it as when, by contact with wet earth, a 'Monday shirt' becomes dirtied or soiled. The more ordinary meaning is of course also used, as when our hill-men on a clean sandy soil speak of their neighbours on the clay weald, a few miles to the south, as 'down in the dirt.'

And this makes me think of door-scrapers. Throughout the clay weald, at the doors of churches and of houses of all classes, may be found iron door-scrapers of many a good pattern; while at many cottage doors is a birch scraper, looking like a large birch broom anchored to the ground by having its handle driven through it into the earth. It is a capital scraper and easily made, by first driving in a strong and fairly long stake, and then binding on some stiff birch spray with hazel withes. You hold on to the top of the stake while you scrape off the mud.

To go back to the old people's words. The great piles of cumulus cloud that are about in thundery weather are called 'thunder-pillars.'

The letter 'b' is often softened into 'v'; as in 'disturve' for 'disturb,' and 'root fivres' for 'root fibres.'

Green vegetables were generically known as 'sauce.' A labourer with a productive garden is said to have 'a nice bit of ground to grow sauce in.'

An interesting case of phonetic evolution is the country name for the mountain-ash, 'twig-bean.' An old English name for this tree, which grows commonly in the neighbourhood, is 'quick-beam' or 'quicken-beam.' Possibly the transition from beam to bean has come about from the three-year-old suckers being much sought after as bean-poles. Bean-poles remind one of pea-sticks, locally called 'pea-rises,' but generally pronounced 'pea-rices.'

Junipers, which are wild about the hills, are always 'jinnipers.'

In the case of a name that presents no particular meaning there seems to be a tendency to convert it into something with a sense to it, as in the 'twig-bean.'

A countryman brought me some stewing pears. I asked what he called them.

'Cattle-axe,' he answered.

I thought a moment and then said: 'Oh yes, Catillac, giving the name somewhat the French pronunciation, but, as I thought, suitably anglicised.

'No,' he said; 'Cattle-axe.'

It was so evident that he would not be satisfied without the name suggesting some kind of meaning, that to humour him I said: 'Ah, I suppose they're called Cattle-axe because they're so big and heavy that if a bullock was grazing in an orchard and one came down on his head it would hit him a whack almost like a pole-axe.'

He at once brightened up and said, 'Yes, that's just it.'

'Dew's Ann' (Deux Ans), I have had in a bill for apples.

'Winter-pickets' was an old name for sloes, the fruit of the blackthorn.

Yeast with the older people is still called 'barm,' and faggots are 'bavins,' pronounced 'bahv'n.' A thorn is a 'bush.' They say of a dog limping on three legs, 'He's got a bush in his foot.'

The 'a' is always broad, sometimes very much lengthened or drawn out. Driving along one summer day I came upon the scene of an accident. The tail-board of a farm cart had come out and had let down a tub with a loose cover. The road was covered with a beery-smelling foaming pool.

'What's that?' I asked; 'beer?'

One word alone the carter answered, but he made the most of it—

'BAA-A-A-A-A-RM.'

Twenty was always 'a score' to the old folks; a hen-coop was 'a rip'; five shillings was 'a crown.' Why we have dropped the word 'crown' and yet kept the 'half-crown' it would be difficult to say.

'I be'ant no scholard' means 'I cannot read or write.' Accounts were kept by notches on hazel sticks. The old people never say 'deaf,' always 'hard of hearing.' Forty years ago, when a mischievous boy pulled down or destroyed a bird's nest, he called it 'mucking the nest.' The old woodman spoke of trees that had been drawn up tall and spindly in a thick wood as "drah'd up limmer.'

Feeling unwell was expressed in different ways: 'I'm feeling sadly,' or 'very middling,' or 'not up to much.' Being faint or weak for want of food was expressed as 'I feel a bit leary' or 'lear.' Very near the German *lehr*.

To shut (locally shet) in the sense of joining or fitting together is still used. The blacksmith 'shets' the tire of the wheel; the horse is 'shet' into the cart. He is also 'shet' out. A woman's work carelessly and inefficiently done is 'slummacking': 'She does her work in a slummacking sort of way.'

A BILL ON A HAZEL STICK

To give an ordinary greeting is 'to pass the time of day' or 'give the time of day.' One neighbour who had squabbled with and been cut by another said: 'She passed me by and never so much as' give me the time of day.'

Fern—it is a county of bracken—was always 'farn.' The word so pronounced has passed into place-names, as Farnham and Farncombe, and appears also in personal names.

'Store' is used as a verb in the sense of 'to value,' or, as in old days, 'to set store by.' An old friend, pointing to a little pink-banded basin on her dresser shelf, said, 'That basin was my mother's; I stores that, same as I does everything as was her'n.'

Sure-ly, as an exclamation of surprise, has a strong accent on the second syllable.

The word 'corn' is turned into two distinct syllables, thus, 'coh-wern.'

'Milk' is also made a dissyllable—'may-ulk;' this is almost identical with the Swedish *mjölk*.

'Fast,' in the sense of steady, firm, steadfast, is retained in the old carter's cry in the hay-field, 'Stand fast,' when he is about to move the horses on. It is a warning to the men on the top of the load.

To gobble is to 'gollop.' 'Don't gollop your food' was said to a child who was eating too fast.

The convenient 'anywhen,' a useful companion to 'anywhere and anyhow,' is still in common use among the older people. I have even heard of 'anywhen-abouts.' 'Somewhen' and 'oft-times' are also in use.

'Do I dare do so' meant 'may I do it,' or 'have I leave to do it'—as, 'Please, mother, do I dare go to bed?'

Among the local names of ordinary tools, a pick is always 'peck'; a deep, narrow-bladed spade, used in cutting trenches in stiff soil for laying drain-pipes, is a 'graft'; a digging fork is an 'eevle'—I have never seen the word written, but this is how it sounds.

A stump of a tree that has been cut down is a 'stam.' 'Ship' is the plural of sheep.

A middle-aged or old man of the labouring class is

always spoken of as Master So-and-so. The older people habitually spoke of any squire's wife with the prefix 'Lady' instead of 'Mrs.' It was no confusion of mind about social distinctions, but the custom of the country.

The clock was generally spoken of as 'she': 'she's a bit slow.'

To give a hint or make a suggestion was thus worded. The clergyman was one day surprised and slightly alarmed by a worthy old soul stopping in front of him with a beaming face and pulling up her outer petticoat to reveal a warm red one underneath—the gift of his wife. 'Thank you, sir,' for 'putting it into your lady to give me this beautiful petticoat.'

A word is sometimes used in a sense whose intention it is difficult to make out, as in this authentic instance.

'So you're goin' to buy a pony off Master D., be you. Well, you'd better take care how you deals with he; *he's a very religious man!*'

Sometimes, after a solemn pause, a rejoinder or a supplementary remark is made with an air of profound wisdom, and as if to throw quite a new light on the subject.

Two labourers stood at the edge of a field, some ten feet above a hollow lane, where I was driving, and passing a farm cart, with barely an inch to spare. The cart had stopped and had one wheel already a little way up the steep bank.

'Lane's ter narrer.'

'Yus' (long pause, and then this profound remark); 'it ain't wide enough.'

One day I missed a garden labourer and said to the one who worked with him, 'Where's Jim?'

'Jim, he ain't come this mornin'; he ain't up to much. He's got a colic'—(long and earnest pause)—'in his inside.'

The villagers like to make out what their church bells say, and to poke fun at each other on the subject.

Dunsfold has three bells. They bang out a challenge to the neighbouring villages: 'WHO BEATS WE?' Hascombe, next door to the east, has only two, but found she could answer quite to her own satisfaction: 'WE DO.' Both say that Hambledon, who has only one, dolefully bewails herself: 'A-OH.'

Truculent Dunsfold says of Chiddingfold, which has six bells, that they say 'POOR CHIDD'N FOLD, HUN GRY'AN COLD.' But this is pure envy, for Chiddingfold is a fine large place, quite as well-to-do as any of them.

There are old customs about tolling for a death that are still followed, such as tolling three times three for a man, three times two for a woman, and the small bell for a child; but the details of the custom appear to vary from place to place.

Dunsfold has a favourite saying: 'We won't be druv,' signifying, 'We may be kindly led, but will not be driven.'

A saying, frequent in the district, in praise of a man who is wide-awake or more than ordinarily intelligent is: 'He's got his head screwed on the right way.'

CHAPTER XII

OLD COUNTRY FOLK; SOME OF THEIR WAYS

SOME kind of belief in witchcraft certainly existed among labouring people, at any rate, up to the middle of the nineteenth century. I can well remember how often we used to hear about it when I was a child.

I have tried to gather some details from two or three of my oldest cottage friends, but, either they have nothing to tell me, or they are shy of acknowledging that it was once a belief among them. Only one of them can remember anything at all definite. This was about a witch-woman who gave a girl baby some cakes, the supposed consequence of which was that the child wasted away, its limbs shrinking almost to nothing. The mother said its arms felt like little sticks when it was in bed with her at night.

The continuation of the narrative was so vague and inconsequent that I could make nothing more of it except that the bright idea struck some one that the witch should be paid for the cakes, which would break the spell. Twopence was accordingly sent, *sealed down;* the sealing was considered of great importance.

A quarter of a pound of new pins was boiled with certain ceremonies and incantations, but I could not ascertain how the thing worked; pins were also stuck in doorways. Pins seemed always to figure in these practices, both in the cause of aggressive enmity and in that of defence.

An old custom that I remember in my young days, as a strong expression of public opinion, was the performance of 'Rough music.'

If a man was known to beat his wife, he was first warned. The warning was a quiet one enough — not a word was spoken; but some one went at night with a bag of chaff, and laid a train of it from the roadway up to the cottage door. It meant, 'We know that thrashing is going on here.' If the man took the hint and treated his wife better, nothing more happened. But if the ill-treatment went on, a number of men and boys came some other night with kettles and pans and fire-irons, and anything they could lay their hands on to make a noise with, and gave him 'Rough music.' The din was something dreadful, but the effect was said to be salutary. My home was half a mile from the village, but every now and then on summer nights we used to hear the discordant strains of this orchestra of public protest and indignation.

The daily life of the cottager varied so little in one cottage or another, or in one village or the next, that the usual restriction of ideas and interests was only to be expected; but every now and then it was a pleasure to find some cottage housewife with a distinct taste for some occupation, or a general aptitude for wider interests. Sometimes it was patchwork, or beautiful plain needlework; a thing that by long practice became almost an extra sense. The skill often remained, even when sight was much impaired; and I am told by some one, whose word I absolutely trust, of an old woman who lived on the outskirts of Godalming who could still stitch shirt-fronts when totally blind.

My old friend, ninety years of age, whose portrait

comes presently, though her memory is failing, was a woman of excellent general ability. It was she who described to me the making of rushlights and tinder. When asking her something about women's work on the farms in harvest-time she told me how she 'used to turn the fan, winnowing.' She could not describe the implement quite clearly, but said, 'I'll make you a pattern.' The next time I went to see her she had made this little model with some split sticks, pins, tin-tacks, and string.

The hand winnowing-fan stood on the barn floor. In

Model of Winnowing-Fan

front of it was a sieve, partly supported by an upright stick, worked by a man, while another shovelled the grain into the sieve.

As the man riddled the corn through the sieve, the chaff was blown aside by the wind made by the revolving flaps of stout sacking nailed to the axle of the machine.

'I should like to show you the book I wrote,' she said one day.

'What! you wrote a book?' I said.

She got up—she was sitting on the foot of her bed—

The Cottage Porch

and opened a drawer of her chest of drawers. After a little searching she produced an old penny account-book.

'It's the story of my life,' she said; 'I did mean to fill the book, but I never got no further.'

It was all written in capital letters with a dot carefully put between each word. For all its odd childishness

The Writer of the Autobiography

there was something about it that seemed to give so pleasant an idea of the simple happiness and contentment of rural life in the early nineteenth century, that I copied it out just as it was, and photographed two pages.

```
WHEN · I · WAS · A · LITTEL · GIRL ·
THE · TROUTH · TO · YOU · I · TELL ·
I · LIVED · WITH · MY · DEAR ·
FRENS · A · TOME · THEY
KEAP · A · LITTEL · COW · AND
I · CANNOT · TELL · YOU ·
HOW · I · IN · JOYED · A · RON ·
TO · FICH · HER · HOME
```

YES · I · LIVED · WITH · MY
DEAR · FRENS · SO · KIND
THEN · THE · COW · WENT
OUT · TO · GRASS · AND ·
THE · TIME · SO · MERRELY
PAST · WHEN · I · WENT
IN · THE · COMMON
HER · TO · FIND

MY · FATHER · WHENT · A · WAY ·
TO · HES · LABOUR · ALL · THE · DAY
WHILE · MY · MOTHER · ALL · HER ·
WORK · DID · DO · A · TOME · AND ·
THE · PUDING · WAS · SO · NIES ·
THAT · WAS · MEAD · WITH ·
MILK · AND · RICE · DOUNT · YOU
THINK · THAT · I · HAD · A · GOOD · HOME

IT · WAS · THEN · A · GOOD · LIVING
THEY · DID · GET · AND · IT · WAS ·
BY · THE · SEET · OF · THER ·
BROW · MY · KIND · FRINES ·
I · NEVER · CAN · FORGET
AND · IT · WAS · WHEN · THY ·
KEEP · THAT · LITTEL · COW ·

IT · WAS · THEN · I · LIVED · HAPPY
AND · FREE · THEN · THE ·
BUTTER · WAS · SENT · TO
SHOP · AND · SOME · OTHER
GOODS · WE · GOT · THE · TIME
AGINE · I · NEVER · MORE
SHELL · SEE ·

THEN · SOME · PIGS · THEY · DID
KEEP · TO · MAKE · THER · OWN ·
MEAT · AND · THERE · GARDENES ·
WELL · STORED · WITH · CORN ·
THEY · MADE   THER · OWN
BRED · WITH · THER · OWN
GROWN · WETE · TWAS · BEFOR
MY · YOUNGS · SISTER · WAS · BORN

OLD COUNTRY FOLK

AND · THEN · MY · FATHER · THOUGHT ·
HE · WOLD . BELD . A · LITTEL .
COT · AND · TO · WHICH · THEN ·
HE · SOON · DID · BEGIN · BUT ·
MY · FATHERS · HALTH · DID · (NT
FEAIL · AND · IT · BLUE · A · DIFFERE
GALE · BEFORE · HE · GOT · IT ·
REDEY · TO · LIVE · IN

AND·THEN·MY·FATHER·THOUGHT
HE·WOLD·BELD·A·LITTEL·
CCT·AND·TO·WHICH·THEN·
HE·SOON·DID·BEGIN·BUT·
MY·FATHERS·HALTH·DID·(NT
FEAIL·AND·IT·BLUE·A·DIFFERE
GALE·BEFORE·HE·GOT·IT
REDEY·TO·LIVE·IN

MY·FATHER·SAID·ONE·DAY·
HE·WAS·GOING·A·LITTLE·WAY
I·MUST·STAY·AT·TOME·HE·WOLD·
NOT·BE·LONG·BUT·I·NEW
THAT·HE·WAS·LERE·AND·I
AFTER·HIM·DID·CREEP·FOR
FEAR·HE·WOLD·FOLE·INTO
THE·POOND

MY·MOTHER·WAS·SO·KIND
AND·SHE·NEVER·HAD·A
MIND·A·WAY·THEN·A
GOSPING·TO·ROME·SHE
WORKED·WITH·ALL·HER
MIGHT·AND·IT·WAS·HER·
HARTS·DELIGHT·TO·BE·WITH
HER·CHILDRING·AT·TOME

I·DHUGED·HIM·A·LONG·TILL
MY·MOTHER·HE·MAT·WILE
THE·LITTLE·ONES·I·LEFT
THEM·A·LONE·SHE·SAD·MY
DEARESTDEAR·HOW·COULD
YOU·WONDER·HEAR
I·AM·A·FREAD·THAT·YOU
NEVER·WILL·GET·HOME

THE MANUSCRIPT

MY · MOTHER · WAS · SO · KIND
AND · SHE · NEVER · HAD · A
MIND · A · WAY · THEN · A
GOSPING · TO · ROME · SHE
WORKED · WITH · ALL · HER · MIGHT
AND · IT · WAS · HER ·
HARTS · DELIGHT · TO · BE · WITH ·
HER · CHILDRING · AT · TOME

MY · FATHER · SAID · ONE · DAY ·
HE · WAS · GOING · A · LITTLE · WAY
I · MOST · STAY · AT · TOME · HE · WOLD
NOT · BE · LONG · BUT · I · NEW
THAT · HE · WAS · WEKE · AND · I
AFTER · HIM · DID · CREP · FOR
FEAR · HE · WOLD · FOLE · IN · TO ·
THE · POOND

I · DHUGED · HIM · A · LONG · TILL
MY · MOTHER · HE · MAT · WILE
THE · LITTLE · ONES · I · LEFT ·
THEM · ALONE · SHE · SAID · MY
DEAREST · DEAR · HOW · COULD
YOU · WONDER · HEAR
I · AM · A · FREAD · THAT · YOU
NEVER · WILL · GET · HOME

AND · THEN · MY · MOTHER · SEAD
YOUR · TIRED · I · AM · AFREAD ·
TO · CARRY · YOU · IT · IS · MY
GOOD · WILL · NOW · YOU ·
MAY · THINK · IT · QUER · BUT
AS · TRUE · AS · I · AM · HERE ·
SHE · CARRIED · HIM · ON · HER
BACK · UP · THE · HILL ·

THEN · MY · FATHER · DIED ·
AND · WE · ALL . BETTERLY · CRID ·
BUT · MY · MOTHER · SED · IT · IS · THE ·
LORDS · WILL · SO · MY · BROTHER
SED · IEL · WORK · THEN · MY ·
FATHERS · PLES · TO · FELL ·
SO · A · WEY · THEN · WE · WENT ·
LIKE · TO · DOVES · HAPPY · AS ·
THT · KING · AND · QUIN ·
OF · IN · THE · MORNING · AT ·
6 · AND · HOME · AT · NIGHT · AT · 9 ·

The ending is a little abrupt and disdainful of both rhyme and rhythm.

They worked long hours in those old days, children and all. Children of six and seven years of age were employed on the farms, just as they were fifty years before. An example of such children's work is given in the case of William Cobbett, who was a West Surrey man, born near Farnham in 1762. A 'Life of William Cobbett,' published in 1835, says that he 'was employed at a very early age in driving the small birds from the turnip seed, and the rooks from the peas. His next employment was weeding wheat, and leading a single horse at harrowing barley. Hoeing peas followed, and hence he arrived at the honour (to use his own words) of joining the reapers at harvest, driving the team and holding the plough. William and his brothers were strong and laborious, and their father used to boast, with honest pride, that the eldest boy, who was then but fifteen, did as much work as any three men in the parish of Farnham.'

I can remember quite small boys scaring birds in the fields—'Keeping the crows' or 'minding the crows' it was called.

The children were better disciplined and therefore better mannered in these old, hard-working days. Boys in a labourer's family, when a meal was ready, having made themselves clean, stood in a row while grace was said, and did not sit down till they were told.

'I mind when we always ate off wooden trenchers, not crockern plates,' said one of my old friends. 'When we used to have a meat pudden, it was boiled in a pudden cloth, not in a basin as now. There was meat and vegetables and all inside. Each child got a piece of the pudden (the paste), some of the vegetables and some gravy. The meat was kept for next day. It was just the same in the farms, the children didn't dare sit down till they was told.'

Children had not so much playtime in the older days, but girls had more than boys. When several were together they formed a ring and played by various rules. The simplest form of game I remember was played by a ring of children sitting on the grass. One stood out in the middle and gave the signal to the others, who all imitated what she did. The leader would stand up and raise her arms, and wave them up and down three times. Then she would sit down and rock her body three times to and fro. After a few such antics, the last of them in a sitting position, she would jump up and twirl round and sit down again quickly. This was really pretty, and was considered the crowning moment and great joke of the whole game, and was often repeated during its progress.

The farmers were very strict about men coming to their time in the morning. If a man came late he lost a quarter of the day's pay; very likely he was told he was not wanted at all that day. Labourers' wages were thirteen to sixteen shillings a week, but then the rent of a cottage was only two shillings. This makes nearly the same average of proportion between rent and wages as now; the usual reckoning being that one day's wages pays the weekly rent. But in the old days, in the smith's, carpenter's, and other trades, they worked six days in the week; now they only work five.

Fifty years ago mechanics earned from eighteen to twenty shillings for a week of six days, labourers ten to thirteen shillings, farm hands eight to ten shillings, women for field work, eightpence a day. Mechanics now earn from thirty-three to forty-two shillings for a week of five days, labourers eighteen to thirty shillings, farm labourers thirteen to sixteen shillings.

Farmers used to hire their men by the year, but they would discharge them two days before the year was up so that they could not 'claim the parish.' In this way the farmer escaped some payment of rates.

It was wonderful how labouring people contrived to live in the earlier part of the nineteenth century, with their low wages, and the price of bread at one time up to tenpence and even a shilling for the four-pound loaf; when the price of wheat ranged from £30 to £36 a load, and even went as high as £40.

In and about the year 1812 a farm labourer had twelve shillings a week. I have a true record of such a one. There were seven mouths to feed. He was paid in wheat. He had to wheel or carry the corn between two and three miles to the mill and bring back the flour. It was then mixed with bran, beans, peas, or anything of the sort that could be obtained, and even then the amount was insufficient. 'We was hungry always—never had a bellyful.'

Yet some of these sparely-fed people were wonderfully strong. An old man spoke proudly of his mother. 'She was a six-foot woman; she could pick up and carry two bags (sacks) of meal, one under each arm; in pattens too!'

Eighty years ago a sack-lifter in Guildford corn-market laid a wager that he would lift a sack of corn in Guildford market and put it down in Farnham market within five hours. The distance is ten miles. A sack of wheat is four bushels and weighs over two hundredweight.

A crowd of people followed him out of Guildford; down the High Street, over the bridge, and up the very steep ascent of the old road on to the Hog's Back. Twice only he put down his burden and rested for twenty minutes; on Guild-down and by the railing of Poyle Park.

He finished well within the time, and as he put down his sack in Farnham market he merely said: 'Well, I won it.' Then, looking round he said, 'Would any one like to lay me I don't take it back?'

Neither men nor women spared themselves as to labour or long hours. I know of a carpenter with his two sons, Godalming men, who finished a fencing job at Portsmouth one evening at half-past five, and walked all night the thirty-seven miles back to Godalming to be ready at the master's place at six the next morning to see about the next job. They not only walked but trundled a hand-cart with their tools, including spades and iron bars. They thought nothing of walking to jobs at Putney, Wimbledon, or Wandsworth.

Mothers of labourers' families were glad to get their girls out at an early age into any respectable family where they would be fed in return for their work.

One old woman that I knew well told me that she went out at the age of twelve.

'It was a carpenter's family,' she said, 'and there was eleven children. Yes, that was my first place, for a year. I didn't get no wages, only my food, one frock and one bonnet, and a shillin' to take home.

'Then I was hired for a year to go to a farm where the master was a widower, and after that at another farm where there was two ladies. They was the particularest ladies I ever knowd. It ud do any girl good to go and live with such as they. There was the oak stairs—it was always a clean pail of water to every two steps; and I'd as much pride in it as they had.

'My wages never got as fur as four pound. Best place I ever lived in was at Mr. Woods's at Hambledon. Quietest and best master I ever lived with. There was the red-brick kitchen-floor. I used to flow he down with a green broom; best of brooms for bricks; makes the floors red. You makes 'em of the green broom as grows on the common. After I left, there was always a bit of green holly at Christmas, and any win'fall apples he always give me. Ah! he was a good master. He minded me when I was married, and time and again he sent me a bit of beef—till he died—and then my beef died.

'One farm I lived in was nigh some rough ground where tramp people lived, and my missis use to send me out with beautiful gruel to the tramp women in the tents when there was a baby come. It was a very old farmhouse where I lived, with gurt beams athurt the ceilin'.

'But Mr. Woods he was the best man. One day after I left him I was at his place, and he had a cold leg of mutton, and what does he do but take a knife and cut'n in two and give me one piece.

'And one time when bread was so dear he says, "Here's a shillin' to get a loaf"—Ah! we soon cut *he* up.

'I'm seventy-six, and some days don't know how to move about. The rheumatics they do crucify me something crool. I says if any one wants to punish me let 'em give me a stoopin' job. It seems to turn my heart upside down.'

Among my earliest country recollections is that of a fine old butcher, who used to go round slaughtering pigs. Some pigs were among our garden economies, and his visits were therefore periodical. Apart from the gruesome duties of his trade he was a genial creature, and we children generally contrived to get a little talk with him. He had

HOG-FORM AND CUTTING-UP KNIFE

a favourite euphemism for sticking or killing a pig: he always called it 'Puttin' a knife in.' 'Where I puts a knife in I gets a pint' was a remark that I remember.

The hog-form, a low oak bench on short legs, played an important part in the later ceremony of scraping off the hair, after the newly-slaughtered animal had been scalded in boiling water, and, again a few days later, when the butcher returned to cut up the carcase.

In buying pigs, or indeed any other stock or produce, unless the purchase was completed at once, it was (and is) customary to pay a shilling down. It is known as 'laying a shilling on the bargain.' The payment of this deposit makes the agreement binding, even if some one 'came along' afterwards and offered a higher price.

Godalming fair-day (February 13) is credited with a mysterious influence on the weather during the next few weeks. The local saying has it that 'If the sun shines before noon on Godalming fair-day, the winter isn't half over.'

A very old saying, whose form of plurals takes one back to the days of Chaucer, goes—

'So many mistes in March
So many frostes in May.'

'Mistes' and 'frostes' must be read as two distinct syllables. Some of the old people still say 'postes' and 'waspes'; also in two syllables.

There is an old belief that pigs can see the wind. It is how the old folks try to account for the restless way they go squeaking and fidgetting about, when they are running loose in the open in windy weather.

A great charm among our older people was their pleasant, cheerful manner. Here and there, of course, there was some one of a dull or surly nature, but such a thing was quite exceptional. Sometimes this love of cheerfulness extended even beyond the grave, as in the case of an old bell-ringer, who left five pounds to be spent among his fellow-ringers when he died. They were to ring a merry peal at his funeral and have a grand supper. 'No muffled bells for me,' he said.

Perhaps there is nothing that diffuses more happiness

in a plain, every-day sort of way, than this habit of cheerfulness. I think it is one of the things that should be taught to children. It is painful to see how many of the faces of quite young children, as well as those of grown-up people, habitually wear a scowl or some other displeasing or disfiguring expression; whereas the rule was, among the old people I remember, and the few of them that remain, as well as among the present-day labouring people who live in the remoter places, and have inherited their ancestors' graces of manner and countenance; that they met each other with a frank, free bearing and a ready smile, as if they unconsciously carried in their minds the fine old bellringer's testamentary injunction: 'No muffled bells for me.'

Fifty years ago the village fair-days were almost the only week-day holidays. Local benefit clubs arranged that these should also be their club-days. In the forenoon all the members marched in procession. headed by a band and banner; a large silk flag with the name of the club painted on it and some devices. These devices, in the case of the club I remember, were two life-sized hands clasped, as an emblem of mutual helpfulness, and a plough; with the motto 'God speed the plough.' The procession passed the forenoon in going round to the houses of prominent residents, who made some addition to the clubs' finances, and spent the afternoon, after dining together, among the booths of the fair.

In some villages the older forms of amusement were of a very rough kind. There was a traditional fight that took place on Whit-Monday, between the Kaffirs—no doubt a quite recent corruption of Cavaliers—of Coneyhurst Hill in the parish of Ewhurst, and the Diamond-topped Roundheads of Rudgwick, a village just over the Sussex border. It always took place at the 'Donkey' inn at Cranleigh.

In former times there were, no doubt, many such fights in different parishes; they served to let off the superfluous youthful steam, that now finds an outlet in cricket and football; but this particular fight between the local Cavaliers and Roundheads was fought on Whit-Monday only.

In the same place there is a saying: 'On Heffel fairday the old woman lets the cuckoo out.' 'Heffel' is Heathfield, showing that the saying had travelled all the length of Sussex to these forest uplands.

The village inn or ale-house was naturally the centre of gossip and general entertainment. When news travelled slowly and there were no cheap newspapers, and but few of the people could read or write, it was the only warm, cheerful place where men could meet and hear or exchange news. Heavy settles stood partly facing the fire, on each side of the wide 'down' hearth, with its fire of logs.

The leaden tobacco-box was on the narrow chimney-shelf. It was variously ornamented, but one I have has bosses of lions' heads at the ends, and a portrait in relief of the Duke of Wellington in his plumed cocked hat on the front; inside, there is a flat piece of sheet-lead with a knob to keep the tobacco pressed close, so as not to dry up.

LEADEN TOBACCO-BOX

Red moreen curtains were drawn over the windows. The firelight played pleasantly upon them inside and made them show a cheerful, welcoming glow to those who passed along the village street.

For the benefit of those who liked a little mild wagering there was sometimes a wooden disk, painted black and with white figures, nailed up to the underside of a joist within the range of the firelight. It had an iron pointer like a clock-hand, that revolved easily upon its centre. Three men would try their luck, spinning the pointer with a hand or stick. The one who made 'the best of three spins' would drink free at his friends' expense, or according to any rule that was agreed on. It is only of late years that this play has been stopped, as an undesirable form of gambling, and the disks taken down.

ON THE PUBLIC-HOUSE CEILING

Some of the old public-house signs, as well as the shop signs, must have been fine things from a decorative point of view. They were not only painted boards, but also of sculptured wood. The bunch of grapes, two feet ten inches high, I remember all my young life hanging outside the Red Lion Inn at Milford.

It is of eighteenth-century work, and was gilt all over. There must have been a large number of clever carvers of this bold kind of work some hundred and fifty years ago, when the sterns and other portions of ships were highly decorated, and some kind of sign swung above the door of every shop. The shoulders of the bunch had evidently perished from exposure to the weather; they were no

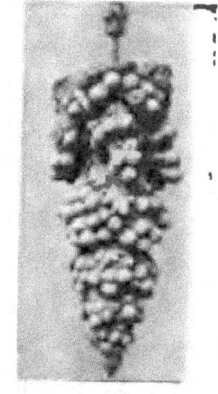

AT THE RED LION

doubt rounded up so as to hide and enclose the bolt that holds the top loop. The iron rod passes right down, and is widened to form the bluntly-pointed tip.

The old ploughman's song is still sung in a neighbouring village, where it has a local record of quite a hundred years. But its age is written in its wording, as may be seen by the now obsolete use of the word 'painful,' which formerly meant industrious or laborious. It was written out by the present singer, and though some of the lines are rugged and their sense obscure, I thought it best to transcribe it faithfully, without attempting to mend the weaker places.

THE PLOUGHMAN'S SONG

COME all you Jolly Ploughmen, with Courage Stout and Bold,
That labours all the Winter in Stormy Winds and Cold,
To clothe the Fields with Plenty, your Farm Yards to renew
To crown them with Contentment behold the painful Plough.

Adam was a Ploughman when ploughing did begin
The next that did succeed him was Cain his eldest Son
None of this generation that's calling now pursue
The Bread that may be wanting remains the painful Plough.

Adam in the Garden was sent to Keep it right
The length of time he stayed there I believe it's said one night
Yet of his own labours I call it not due
For soon he lost his Garden and went and held the Plough.

Oh Ploughman said the Gardener dont count your trade with ours
Walk through the Garden and View the earliest Flowers
Also the curious borders and the pleasant Walks to View
There's not such peace and plenty performed by the Plough.

Behold the welthy Merchant that Trades in Foreign Seas
That brings us Gold and Treasures for those that live at Home at Ease
For we must have Bread and Biscuits Rice Flour Puddings and Peas
To feed our Jolly Sailors, as they Sails on the Seas.

Sampson was the Strongest Man and Soloman was Wise
Alexander for Conqueror was all His daily Pride
King David he was Valliant and many a Thousand Slew
Yet none of His Brave Heroes could live without the Plough.

I hope there is none offended with me for singing this
For it was not intended for any thing amiss
But if considered rightly you will find what I say is true
That the Welth of the Nation depends upon the Plough.

CHAPTER XIII

OLD COUNTRY FOLK—THEIR CLOTHING

AMONG the many changes in ways of living that have come about within the last fifty years, one of the most regrettable is the loss of the characteristic dress of our working folk.

I can just remember when both men and women wore a real country dress. It went on more or less till near 1860, a date when much of the old tradition, in many different ways, was dying. Indeed, I can remember one old man whose Sunday dress was knee-breeches, with a high-collared coat of an almost eighteenth-century type, and a low-crowned beaver hat, and even one who wore a pigtail. This must have been in the fifties.

And there was one old woman whose gown had short sleeves, leaving her arms bare, with which she always wore a blue-checked apron and a large mob-cap. As she worked in her cottage so she went shopping in the village; there was no addition to this costume.

OLD BRASS SHOE-BUCKLES

But the usual women's dress in my youngest days was a print gown and apron, and either a sun-bonnet of cotton print with a deep curtain, or a very plain straw bonnet with a narrower curtain and a single ribbon, that passed over the top and came down to tie under the chin. Often in hay-making or harvesting an old bonnet was worn tipped up almost perpendicularly to shade the eyes. A short handkerchief-shawl covered the shoulders, and a plain large woollen shawl was worn in winter and on Sundays.

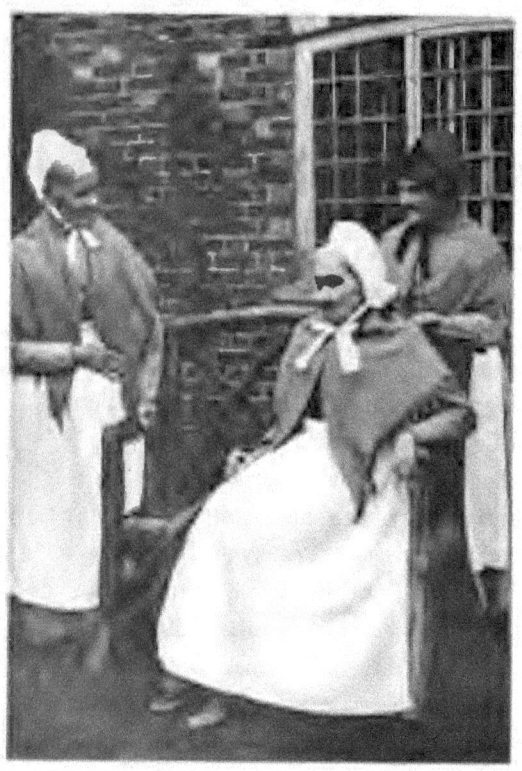

COTTAGERS' DRESS OF 1850

But the pride of the cottager was to have a really good Sunday bonnet. It is shown in the frontispiece. It was invariable in pattern, of black satin, drawn and corded somewhat in the way of a sun-bonnet. After each Sunday's use it was dusted with the greatest care and put away in its band-box. It lasted almost a lifetime.

The Cottage Cap

Closely associated with my recollection of the Sunday bonnet was the custom of carrying the Prayer-book with a

THE PRAYER-BOOK

spray or two of rosemary, southernwood, balm, or some other sweet-smelling herb, and a white handkerchief wrapped round.

AN OLD COTTAGE CAP

The close-fitting muslin cap showed inside the bonnet and was the usual indoor head-dress. The border, of closely-pleated, coarse lace edging, was called the 'front':

THE GARDEN WALL—OUTSIDE

THE GARDEN WALL—INSIDE

the head-piece, the 'caul.' A ribbon went over just behind the front and tied under the chin.

The loss of these white caps is to be sincerely regretted. Clean and tidy in themselves, they were the most charming framing for the honest country faces. As middle and old age came on their fitness was only the more apparent. They gave a dignity to those of middle age, and to old people

THE HEAD-HANDKERCHIEF

a beauty and refinement such as one vainly looks for at the present day. Moreover, they kept the hair in place and preserved it from dust, and were an admirable protection for the head when its natural covering was thin or wanting.

The cotton handkerchief, almost universal on the Continent as a head-covering of women of the peasant class, seems never to have been general in England, though used occasionally, and indeed still used for running out to hang up the wash or some odd job about the garden, as in the case of my friend here depicted. It is a pity that it should not be in general and constant use.

THE SUN-BONNET

Etymology claims such use for it, for the word kerchief is from *couvre chef*, a head-covering.

The sun-bonnet was of some light-coloured print, generally lilac. The making of it is ingenious and pretty, and shows how the older folk took pleasure in doing dainty work. In one that I have the forward part measures $3\frac{1}{2}$ inches from front to back, and consists of thirteen rows of plain cording lying close together. This piece is made separately. Then comes an inch-deep pleated frilling put in full, facing forward and ending in a cording at its back. This cording has a more various and richer appearance than that of the front, as it is done 'full' instead of plain. There are three such lines of 'fulled' frilling and cording, then three more rows of cording, separated by a small space, something less than half-an-inch. Then comes the back, which is formed of the downward gathering together of the stuff to join the top of the curtain.

The curtain has a length of 48 inches, measured along its lower free edge, and comes down to the point of the shoulders. The upper edge is gathered in, to fit the lower edge of the bonnet. It is finished at the back with a flat bow, with ends whose length is the same as the depth of the curtain. There are also strings at the front, which as far as I remember were never tied.

A loose print jacket, open at the front, I am told was worn in the older days, but I have no recollection of having seen it.

Pattens were in general use to near the middle of the last century. They were wooden clogs with a leather toe-piece, and bands of leather that tied with a short lace over the instep. An oval iron hoop, fixed to the under-side, lifted the wearer above the mud.

PATTENS

'Pattens!' said an old friend, when I asked her about them, 'I mind when I always wore 'em, fetchin' water from the well, or any sloppin' about, and I used to get 'em pulled off in the stiff mud down the lane.'

I well remember seeing the sharp prints of the irons on the village footpaths.

My father told me how the sentries at the park gates in London had orders not to allow any one to walk in the park in pattens. It was to prevent the cutting up of the gravel paths.

Children were very simply dressed. Girls had a cotton or stuff frock according to the season, and always a long pinafore. Girls, up to eight or nine years old, had their hair cut short like boys, and wore the same round hats of coarse black felt. Their sleeves were generally short, and their poor little arms uncovered in nearly all weathers.

Boys had short round frocks like small smock-frocks over suits of corduroy; these short frocks were sometimes called by the old name 'gabardine.'

'Let me see,' said my friend the former schoolmistress, 'which boy was it that used always to speak of his gabardine—Was it Jushingto Earl? No, it was Berechiah Gosling.'

The first-named boy's odd Christian name was always a wonder to us as children; the other is a good old Bible name; while 'Gosling,' though to the rustic mind it has a homely connexion, is really a corruption of a grand old French family name. There are many other names in the country of obviously French origin, such as Durrant, which is now almost typically familiar as belonging to West Surrey.

'Berechiah' is evidently a result of the fine old practice of opening the Bible and giving a child a name found on, or close to, the page at which the book was opened. The modern way—comparing very badly with the old—seems to be to give children names out of penny novelettes, or in imitation of the prevalent silly fashion for frivolous fancy names.

The simple and charming dress of young cottage girls of the older time, the cotton print frock,—the long pinafore

THE WHITE SMOCK-FROCK

and the plain sun-bonnet—is delightfully shown in Mrs. Allingham's 'Happy England.'

The old carter's smock-frock or round frock, still lingering, but on its way to becoming extinct, is centuries old. No better thing has ever been devised for any kind of outdoor wear that admits of the use of an outer garment. It turns an astonishing amount of wet, especially when of the ordinary local pattern, shown at p. 219, that has a wide turn-over collar, something like a sailor's, but coming square over the shoulders in front and behind. The frock is cut quite square; of two whole widths of the stuff, with side seams only. The shaping is made by the close

THE WHITE FROCK

gathering, either over the whole back and front, or in two panels on the breast and back near the buttons.

It can be worn either way about; back and front are alike. It sits just as well either way. The sleeves are put in very low; not on the shoulder, but some inches down the arm. There is a worked gathering at their insertion, and also at the wristband, to bring the greater width of the sleeve into the size of the wrist. The material is a strong, tough, closely-woven linen. It was in four colourings; light and dark grey, olive green and white.

A 'best frock,' and a tall hat with long nap, or the usual felt hat, was the Sunday dress, unless a man had a suit of cloth wedding clothes, which would be his Sunday suit for life. For in the old days clothes were made to

AN OLD SUNDAY SMOCK

last, and if a man had such a suit it would never be worn to work in, and a lifetime of Sundays would scarcely wear it out.

It was an old custom for a girl engaged to be married to work a round frock for her future husband, and one can well imagine with what care and pleasure the beautiful patterns would be stitched by the loving fingers.

I can remember when one could tell what a man was

THE BLACKSMITH

by his distinctive dress. How little of this remains; even the red caps of the brewers' vanmen are now but rarely seen.

The smith's leather apron remains, and always must, as it is a need of his work. My friend in the picture wears his shorter than usual; it might have a higher bib. But I can remember a regular carpenter's dress; a short jacket of thick white baize or felt, an apron and a neat paper cap.

Now, alas! all workpeople, except those who do the hardest outdoor labour, such as navvies, stone-pitmen, and farm-labourers, are clothed in a dead-level of shabbiness. The shops are full of cheap suits with a pretence of fashion, which are bought for Sunday wear. They are soon past their best, and are then taken into working use, for which they are entirely unfit. The result is that it is only the farm-labourer and his hard-working kind, who *must* wear the right or suitable kind of clothes, who look well dressed. For real working clothes, like all other things that are right and fit for their purpose, *never look shabby*. They may be soil-stained; they may be well-worn, but they never have that sordid, shameful, degraded appearance of the shoddy modern Sunday suit put to an inappropriate use.

I am not using these words in a spirit of blame, but in one of regret. Working people are tempted by the shops, that present their wares in a convenient and superficially attractive way. I am not even blaming the shopkeepers; they are driven to this way of doing business by the pressure of trade competition. The shops display the attractive thing at a cheap price; the salesman's duty to his employer is to push it.

Unfortunately the word 'fashionable' has an attraction that speaks but ill for the good sense of the buyer of the labouring class.

Lately I was in a draper's shop, where, next to me at the counter, was what I judged to be a labourer's wife. She

SOME OF THE OLD SORT IN WHITE CORDUROY

had asked for white handkerchiefs. Her choice was wavering between two sizes, and seemed inclined for the larger, but she bought a wretched little useless cotton wisp on being assured by the salesman that it was the 'fashionable ladies' size.

Every sort of folly or absurdity is committed by these poor people in this insane striving to be what they think is 'fashionable.' A lamentable example was shown me lately. It was a photograph of a wedding party of the labouring class. The bride had a veil and orange blossoms, a shower bouquet, and *pages!* The bridegroom wore one of the cheap suits aforesaid, and had a billycock hat pushed back from his poor, anxious, excited face that glistened with sweat. In his buttonhole was a large bouquet, and on his hands *white cotton gloves!* No more pitiful exhibition could well be imagined.

Have these poor people so utterly lost the sense of the dignity of their own position that they can derive gratification from the performance of such an absurd burlesque? Such wedding parties do not walk to church: the bride's party, at least, hires the closed village fly, which for the occasion is called 'the brougham.'

A wise old woman remarked, 'When *I* was married we walked to church; and then walked home, and I cooked two chops. And then we changed our clothes and went to our work!'

Gipsy folk and other wandering van people kept to their picturesque red head-handkerchiefs and great gold earrings to a comparatively late date; but the great wave of ill-taste has engulfed them too, and of late years they have worn ulsters with aprons outside, and battered hats with broken, rusty ostrich feathers!

The ploughman and farm-labourer still wear the capital white slop jacket in summer. They unconsciously regret the knee-breeches of their ancestors, for they strap their cord trousers round below the knee.

OLD COUNTRY FOLK

It is a pleasure when one still sees a good countrywoman's face with the hair worn in the plain old way—not tousled into an untidily frizzled fringe.

Sometimes, though always more rarely, one sees at a railway station a good old body with her light load of

THE PLAIN OLD WAY

luggage done up in the nice old way in clean cotton handkerchiefs.

These large blue and white handkerchiefs may still be bought at the ready-made clothing shops in country towns. Fifty years ago, when paper was much less cheap and plentiful, they were more used for carrying purposes. Country women shopping, were always provided with them, as well as with a capacious basket.

Labouring men had the bread and meat they carried for their dinner, in a clean handkerchief, inside the rush dinner-basket. Now it is taken, for the most part, in a

LUGGAGE FOR A JOURNEY

COLOURED COTTON HANDKERCHIEFS

piece of newspaper, and the paper is thrown away by the side of the road.

Some of the patterns of these cotton handkerchiefs are shown in the illustration. Their colouring is almost always red and white, red and buff-yellow with a little black, or blue and white. They are still to be had, and are commonly used as pocket-handkerchiefs by labourers, but their old use for wrapping and carrying is now but little seen.

CHAPTER XIV

COTTAGE GARDENS

COTTAGE folk are great lovers of flowers, and their charming little gardens, in villages and by the roadside, are some of the most delightful incidents of road-travel in our southern counties.

The most usual form of the cottage flower-garden is a strip on each side of the path leading from the road to the cottage door. But if the space is a small one it is often all given to flowers. Sometimes, indeed, the smaller the space the more is crammed into it. One tiny garden, that I used to watch with much pleasure, had nearly the whole space between road and cottage filled with a rough staging. It was a good example of how much could be done with little means but much loving labour. There was a tiny green-house, of which the end shows to the left of the picture, that housed the tender plants in winter, but it could not have held anything like the quantity of plants that appeared on the staging throughout the summer. There were hydrangeas, fuchsias, show and zonal geraniums, lilies and begonias, for the main show; a pot or two of the graceful francoa, and half-hardy annuals cleverly grown in pots; a clematis smothered in bloom, over the door, and, for the protection of all, a frame-work, to which a light shelter could be fixed in case of very bad weather.

It must have given pleasure to thousands of passers-by;

'My Cluster-Rose do blow beautiful'

A Staging of Pot-Plants

CLUSTER ROSE IN A COTTAGE GARDEN

COTTAGE GARDENS

to say nothing of the pride and delight that it must have been to its owner.

There is scarcely a cottage without some plants in the window; indeed, the windows are often so much filled up with them that the light is too much obscured. The wise cottagers place them outside in the summer, to make fresh growth and gain strength.

These window plants are the objects of much care, and often make fine specimens. The cactus, whose owner is tying it up with a bit of soft thread, stood in the cottage window that was thickly embowered by a banksia rose in unusually full bloom.

The old double white rose, brother of the pretty pink Maiden's Blush, never seems so happy or looks so well as in a cottage garden; and the old kinds of cluster roses are great favourites.

THE WINDOW PLANT

The deep-rooting Everlasting Pea (Winter-bean is its local name) is a fine old cottage plant, and Nasturtiums ramble far and wide. Nowhere else does one see such Wallflowers, Sweet-Williams, and Canterbury Bells, as in these carefully-tended little plots.

It is a sign of careful gardening and good upbringing, when the little boys of a family are seen on the roads with old shovels and little improvised hand-carts, collecting horse-droppings. It means that the plants will have a nourishing surface mulching, that will be much to their benefit.

China Asters are great favourites—'Chaney Oysters' the old people used to call them—and Dahlias, especially the tight, formal show kinds, are much prized and grandly grown.

Sweet-smelling bushes and herbs, such as rosemary, lavender, southernwood, mint, sage, and balm, or at least some of them, were to be found in the older cottagers'

ROSES AND CANTERBURY BELLS

garden plots. Perhaps southernwood was the greatest favourite of all. An old man said that when he was young he used to put bergamot (Monarda) into his hair-grease—'Just did please the girls,' he said.

Here and there is a clipped yew over a cottage entrance; but this kind of work is not so frequent as in other parts of the country.

COTTAGERS AND THEIR POT-PLANTS

BANKSIAN ROSE ROUND A COTTAGE WINDOW

CLUSTER ROSE ON A COTTAGE ENTRANCE

THE EVERLASTING PEA AT A COTTAGE DOOR

A Cottager's Border of China Asters

Dahlias in the Cottage Garden

These little gardens always seem to me to speak of the joy of life and cheerfulness of disposition, that are such

CLIPPED YEWS AT A COTTAGE ENTRANCE

fine attributes of the character of our genuine country folk. It was more clearly shown two generations ago, when men's lives were less hurried and more concentrated, and when the simple country life was fuller and more satisfying.

CHAPTER XV

FOUND IN THE WOODS

VARIOUS old things, relics of more barbarous days, are from time to time found in the woods.

The large spring-trap, of a size for a fox or an otter, probably dates from the beginning of the last century. It

OTTER OR FOX-TRAP, TOASTING-FORK, AND BAKING-IRON

is of the same construction as the ordinary vermin-trap, but much larger, its length being two feet four inches.

I cannot let pass the subject of these traps without expressing my horror and detestation of the cruelties that go on in the woods around us; cruelties that I cannot but think are absolutely unwarranted by any needs or

FOUND IN THE WOODS

interests of game preservation. The pain and terror occasioned by actual shooting are bad enough, but I cannot understand how the frightful tortures inflicted by traps, can, on any grounds whatever, be justified to the consciences of the many otherwise estimable and humane people who consent to their use.

Spring-guns still occasionally come to light in the

SPRING-GUNS

woods. The spring-gun was not generally intended to shoot the poacher, but to make known his presence in the woods to the keeper. The usual shape was a short barrel in which the charge was placed. At its base is a nipple for a percussion-cap. A powerful striker is held suspended over the cap by a short bar, which, with three longer bars, is supported by a pivot on which they turn. Wires, stretching across the ride or path through the covert, are attached to the longer bars. When one of these is struck by the poacher or trespasser the short bar is released; it falls on the cap and explodes the charge. A sheet-iron cover protects it from the weather. In the illustration the complete spring-gun is the one lying on the bench. It was used the other way up, the mouth of the barrel facing the ground, but raised a little way above the ground at the barrel end by a short stump for the square nib beyond the barrel to rest on.

But they were also used set horizontally, and with a shotted charge, with the intention of injuring the poacher.

Such use of spring-guns, also the use of man-traps, was made illegal in the year 1861, though notices of such dangers were posted on the outsides of plantations to within a comparatively recent date. At the present day it is legal to set a spring-gun *inside* a dwelling-house and at night only. As alarm-guns they may be used with blank charge, set vertically to explode either upward or downward, but set horizontally and charged they are illegal.

Dog-spears were set in the woods. They were sharply-pointed iron rods, three to four feet long, fixed in wooden sockets, also pointed to go into the ground. They were set at an angle of forty-five degrees in the grassy covert paths, and either speared a poacher through the legs, or ran a dog through the chest as he raced down after a rabbit.

A neighbouring squire set lines, with large fish-hooks attached, across the rides in his coverts. The poachers came, the lines were found broken and many hooks gone. The poachers did not go that way again! But it was a barbarous thing to do.

FOUND IN THE WOODS

A large man-trap was found about forty years ago in a wood within a mile and a half of my home. It now hangs, as a curious relic of cruel old days, over the door of a smith's and wheelwright's shop.

The finding of it, apart from its own interest, had its

THE MAN-TRAP

humorous side, for it was discovered in a wood on a beautiful property owned by a lady who had four then unmarried daughters. Luckily, no one enjoyed the obvious joke more than these dear ladies themselves; kindest and best of neighbours, of whom, alas! only one now survives.

CHAPTER XVI

GODALMING

GODALMING was a very quiet, almost sleepy, little town, from the time when coaching was killed by the railways up to about the year 1860.

The building of the Charterhouse School, finished in 1872, did much to awaken it, and to raise the value of land in the immediate neighbourhood for building. It also gave a lively impetus to trade; and Godalming is now as flourishing and commercially active a town as any of its size in the south of England. About the same time, too, the neighbouring country was, one may say, discovered, and land values rose largely, though not as yet to their present very high rate. Godalming's busy little High Street has lost somewhat of its older character, yet enough remains—and long may it be preserved—to remind one of its life and history for the past three centuries and even more.

What was most apparent, before the change to its present vitality, was a certain air or atmosphere of the older life of the coaching days.

The greater part of the north side of Bridge Street was still occupied by a range of old half-timbered buildings dating at least from Stuart times. Some would be of much greater antiquity, if the name 'King John's Palace,' which hung about one of them, that had a quadrangle within, could claim historical accuracy.

The name 'Bridge Street' is itself modern, for there

THE 'WHITE HART' INN

are some yet living who remember it as 'Water Street'; when there was no bridge over the Wey, and coaches, road-waggons, and all wheeled traffic passed through the river by a ford; a slight wooden foot-bridge carrying those who walked. A little further along, on the Guildford side,

OLD HOUSES IN THE HIGH STREET

a lesser ford crossed a small back-water or meadow drain. The bridge was built in 1782.

Godalming High Street presents an unusually interesting sequence of examples of local architecture.

There is the old timber-framed inn, the 'White Hart,' that must be a relic from the sixteenth century or even earlier, and a timber-framed building at the beginning of Church Street, and smaller examples of the same in Church Street itself; and, in the High Street, some excellent brick houses, one block of which is dated 1663.

GODALMING

But I think it is the brick buildings of the town, of a later date, that give the street its more distinct character, and foremost among these are some of the inns that played so important a part in its life before the days of railways; during the eighteenth, and nearly throughout the first half of the nineteenth centuries. The most important of these, architecturally, are the very large inn—the 'King's Arms,' the 'Great George,' and the 'Little George.'

The 'Little George' seems to me to be a quite unusually satisfactory example of street architecture; of excellent proportion, of sufficient ornament, all derived from or growing out of its structure, and in all ways just what a street house in such a town should be. It is dignified and yet modest; in perfect taste, and therefore commanding one's unstinted admiration. It might serve well as a model, not necessarily for actual imitation, but for safe guidance, in the case of new buildings that have to be erected.

THE 'LITTLE GEORGE' INN

Recently there has been a rather warm discussion about the little Town Hall at the western end of the High Street. There was a strong feeling among one section of influential townsmen that it should be removed, as an obstruction to traffic. I am truly thankful, for the sake of the honour and good taste of Godalming, that the better counsel, for its preservation, has prevailed. The argument against it was that it was neither beautiful nor particularly useful, and very much in the way. Perhaps it is not exactly beautiful, but its slender-pillared little clock-tower and copper-sheathed cupola are distinctly good, and I believe it to be the latest building in Godalming that has that precious quality of *character*—a thing that can scarcely be defined, but that is most clearly perceptible to all who have sympathy with the history of the place as shown in its architectural expression.

The removal of this landmark of the early days of the nineteenth century would be a grievous injury to the town.

It is very easy to see the question from the other point of view, but this view can only be entertained by those who are not, either by education or by such God-given aptitude or insight, fostered by certain other lines of education, quite in a position to form a critical judgment in the matter.

Even from the point of view of commercial convenience and well-being it would be well if there could be some strict censorship exercised in the matter of the removal or rebuilding of houses in such conspicuous positions as the streets of country towns.

I venture to affirm that the possession of beautiful old houses, and of buildings not perhaps beautiful, but of distinct architectural interest, is an important asset, even from the commercial point of view, of such a town as Godalming. They attract more people of a good class to the town than many of those who contemn them may be aware of. If Godalming is ill-advised enough to destroy the Town Hall, or others of its interesting buildings, or to overload the street with architectural monstrosities so much out of scale that its good old houses are dwarfed and overpowered, the day will come when people of the better sort will say: 'Oh, Godalming is spoilt; we will go somewhere else.'

The common cry is that commercial advancement cannot be barred by merely sentimental objections. After all, in comparison with commerce, what are trifles like love and loyalty, honour and honesty, religion and patriotism, but sentimental? Are they the less powerful agents in moving the minds of men or forming the history of nations? There are a great many people who see no use in the British Museum or the National Gallery, and yet they do not venture to protest against having to pay for their maintenance. These are not commercial institutions, but even those who do not feel the want of them are yet dimly conscious that they are desirable possessions for a great nation.

So it is that those who lately saved the Town Hall, and also Eashing Bridge, deserve well of their country, and have shown the truest patriotism as well as the truest local wisdom. The older buildings, down to the very latest that shows the continuity of architectural progression, are a precious heritage, belonging in a way to the town and county. To retain them untouched, and to preserve them from decay or demolition, should be felt to be the duty of every good townsman.

I feel sure that in another hundred years this will be known more widely and felt more strongly even than now. As we now so keenly regret that want of just appreciation of a hundred years ago that destroyed numbers of those dwellings of Tudor and Stuart times, whose fewer remnants are now so jealously preserved and so worthily prized; and as all educated people unite in condemning the acts of their destroyers; so let us beware, lest our great grandchildren may in like manner be able to say of us: 'What Goths those ancestors of ours must have been!'

Let us hope that the fine old 'King's Arms' inn may stand untouched for another century or two. Here again is a structure that cannot be called beautiful, but that is full of character. It is a large, plain-faced, three-storied brick building, with a simple pediment; and a modest porch on two columns, surmounted by a balcony with plain iron railings. Ten windows in the first floor show to the street front, and a large arch leads to the ample stable-yard.

The 'King's Arms'

It was the great posting inn. The landlord had a farm close by at Farncombe, where from thirty to forty horses were kept. Some of the coaches stopped at this inn, though not so many as were served by the other chief inns of the day. These were the 'Richmond Arms,' the 'Red Lion,' the 'Angel,' and the 'White Hart.'

The local London coach, the 'Accommodation,' here had its home terminus. It ran between Godalming and the 'White Horse,' Piccadilly. The fare was half-a-guinea. It was driven by Chilman, by Dean, and by Scarlet in succession—names well known or remembered in Godalming. It changed horses at Ripley. The horses rested there, and brought the coach back to Godalming in the afternoon.

Many of the long-distance coaches changed at Guildford; and ran through, or only deposited travellers, in Godalming. After Godalming, the Portsmouth to London coaches, which had already changed at Petersfield on the way up, changed again, either at the 'Mariners' at Ripley, at the 'White Lion' at Cobham, or at the 'Bear' at Esher.

A midnight coach from London sometimes brought gangs of convicts, chained together, bound for Portsmouth. They stopped at the 'Red Lion,' where the men got down and had something to eat, as Godalming is nearly half-way between London and Portsmouth. Three miles to the west, a milestone shows the same figure for mileage on both faces of the stone.

But oftener the convict coaches would drive into the large yard of the 'King's Arms,' the gates would be closed, and the armed guards would let their charges out for a short rest and some food. These were gangs of prisoners for transportation; Portsmouth being then the port of embarkation.

If the old 'King's Arms' had kept a register of the important people who passed a night, or who stopped there for lunch or dinner, it would have included many notable names—among them those of the allied sovereigns early in the nineteenth century.

In the Bodleian Library at Oxford is preserved the reckoning of the landlord of the 'King's Arms,' when Peter the Great and his suite—twenty in all—spent a day on the way to Portsmouth.

At breakfast, they consumed half a sheep, half a lamb, ten pullets, twelve chickens, seven dozen eggs, and the contents of two large salad beds; washed down by a gallon of brandy and two gallons of mulled claret.

At dinner, a few hours later, they devoured three stone weight of ribs of beef, a fat sheep, a lamb, two loins of veal, eight capons, ten rabbits, three dozen of sack and a dozen of Bordeaux!

Truly, if old John Evelyn's servant described the barbarous ways of these Russian visitors to his master's place at Deptford as 'right nasty,' he might equally have called their feeding at Godalming 'right gluttonous.'

Another interesting record of the manner in which the air of Godalming stimulated ravenous appetite in persons of high degree reads thus:—

'About fifty years ago, two English dukes stopped at this inn to change horses. Two mutton-chops and a bottle of claret were taken out, which they ate sitting in the carriage. But either the fare was so good or the dukes were so hungry, that they did not proceed till they had devoured thirty-six chops and quaffed ten bottles of claret.'

This paper may presumably have been written about the year 1840, though it is not dated; neither is the identity of the dukes disclosed.

Let us hope that the 'King's Arms' keeps up its character as to the appetising quality of the products of its kitchen and cellar.

In the old days it was no uncommon thing to see a coach carrying sixteen jolly sailors—four inside and twelve out—paid off from a man-of-war that had been three or four years at sea, on their way to London to spend their money. But, as one of my old friends said significantly:

'You would see them walk back!' They carried a good store of liquor to keep up their spirits during the long journey. One sees such jovial parties, depicted by Cruikshank; brandishing the stumpy-shaped bottles, some of which are shown in the illustration.

Such loads of seafaring men sometimes proved a danger to the coaches. They were so much accustomed to being swung about in boats, that, when the coach lurched and swayed on a bad bit of road, or coming downhill, they let

GLASS BOTTLES OF A HUNDRED YEARS AGO

themselves go and swayed with it, instead of following the landsman's instinct of poising the body to counteract the movement of the carriage. Coaches have been overturned from this cause.

Relics of the frequent passing of sailors have remained in the old town. The carving of cocoa-nuts was a favourite occupation on long voyages. The patterns on two of the examples illustrated show a fine feeling for decorative design. On one of them some radiating, fan-shaped flutings leave a few spaces filled with various devices, such as a crown, a fish, and a zigzag pattern. This nut also bears the sailor's name, Laurance Bryon, and the date 1786. The three dark marks at the end, one of them bored out, natu-

CARVED COCOA-NUTS

rally suggest eyes and mouth, and the projection at the same end was ready for the shaping of a blunt nose.

The smaller nut has a ruder ornament, and is of a paler

SPANISH DEMIJOHN

brown colour; the two larger are a rich, deep brown, almost black, with a polish that is lustrous though not actually shining.

Another relic of the sailors is a Spanish demijohn—a very large wicker-covered bottle, longer than wide, and measuring seventeen inches the longest way.

GODALMING

The fact of this road being the main highway to the great southern seaport is also recorded in the signs of many of the inns all the way down from London. The 'Anchor' is frequent; the 'Mermaid,' the 'Mariners,' and the 'Ship' are all well-known signs, and there are probably others.

Separate coaches passed through Godalming from Chichester, Midhurst, Petersfield, Portsmouth, Bognor, and Littlehampton. A well-known figure on the road was Francis Faulkner, who drove the Portsmouth and London coach for fifty years. He was a very stout man, and earned the nickname 'Puffing Billy' from a trick he had

FLINT-LOCK BLUNDERBUSS

of puffing out his cheeks when he pulled up his horses. Early in the eighteenth century the guard of the coach used to be armed with a flint-lock blunderbuss, but later with pistols, that were always called 'bulldogs.' There were long stretches of lonely waste on the Portsmouth road, and they had to be prepared for occasional meetings with highwaymen.

Most of the fish for the London market was conveyed in special fish-vans from the various sea-coast places, such as Littlehampton, Bognor, Emsworth, and Havant. They were painted yellow and had four horses. But some of it, as well as supplies for other inland places, was carried in little carts drawn by dogs.

The dogs were big strong Newfoundlands. Teams of two or four were harnessed together. The team of four would carry three to four hundredweight of fish, besides the driver.

The man would 'cock his legs up along the sharves,' as an old friend describes it, and away they would go at a great rate. They not only went as fast as the coaches, but they gained time when the coach stopped to change horses, and so got the pick of the market. A dog-drawn cart used to bring fish from Littlehampton to Godalming, where oysters were often to be bought for three a penny. A fish-cart man whose name was Jennivary had his house of call in Rock Place.

Then there were the carriers' carts, also drawn by dogs. One of these I well remember, plying between Bramley and Guildford.

In these old days the great road waggons, drawn by six horses, went their long-distance journeys, carrying cattle and sheep to the London market, and bringing back loads of groceries and whatever was wanted. One of these went twice a week between Chichester and London. Besides these there were numbers of the carriers' one-horse vans such as still go short journeys between villages and country towns.

Now the carriers carry note-books, but the older men, who could neither read nor write, could *remember*, and would fill their vans with their many commissions without forgetting anything or making a mistake.

Godalming had formerly a large interest in the wool industry. Thousands of sheep were pastured on the heathy commons, where they contrived to pick up a living, and many of the townspeople were engaged in manufacturing the wool from the raw material to the finished article. Warm woollen clothing was largely made for export to Canada, as well as numbers of articles for the home trade. Among these were the tilts for the great road-waggons, all of wool in the older days. A woolsack appears on the arms of both Guildford and Godalming, and the 'Woolpack' occurs more than once as the sign of an inn in and around the town.

There were also three large breweries in Godalming, in Bridge Street. Barley was grown on the near farms, malted in the town, and hops came from the Farnham district; the nearest being grown at Puttenham.

When some excavations were being made in Bridge Street a few years ago, a quantity of rough tree trunks were found at a depth of seven feet from the surface, showing how provision had been made for a firm foundation for the road, in what had been treacherous ground full of water.

In a book such as this it may seem ungracious to say nothing about beautiful old Guildford, but the subject is too large, and has already been ably treated.

CHAPTER XVII

CHURCHYARDS THEN AND NOW

NOTHING is more noticeable among one's recollections of the changes that have passed over the country than those that have affected our churchyards.

Although, during the last fifty years, the clergy have become much more active and hard-working in all matters connected with the religious and social well-being of their parishes, elements of unrest have crept into our beautiful country churchyards; places that, till the later middle of the last century, had retained their character as 'haunts of ancient peace.'

It is just that quality of peace, and quiet beauty, that all persons, of a reasonable degree of education and refinement, desire to retain about the last place of earthly repose of their dear dead, and it is just this most precious quality of which our churchyards are being despoiled.

Of all places in the world, they are those in which cheap things from the shop are most painfully jarring and out of place; to say nothing of many things which are by no means cheap, but that are thoroughly ill-designed, and totally wanting in both dignity and repose.

In the older days, monuments in country churchyards, erected to the memory of people of means and of some importance of standing, were specially designed by a competent architect. Often they took the form of fine altar-tombs — monuments of much dignity; excellent in

CHURCHYARDS THEN AND NOW 297

proportion, with sufficient and well-placed ornament and well-drawn mouldings.

Even the humblest graves of all, where no stone or lasting memorial was ever to be placed, were more carefully covered with turf than they are now, and the newly-laid turfs were bound with hazel or osier withes crossing

THE OLD ALTAR-TOMB

each other diagonally, with wooden pegs, where one withe passed over the other.

Graves of people of a middle class had head and foot-stones; the head-stone either plain as to its face or with some ornamental carving in low relief; but usually with the upper line pleasantly treated in one or two traditional ways.

The monuments, if any, to members of the labouring class, or people who could not well afford stone, were the dignified but unpretentious grave-boards. Each district had a traditional pattern of finial at the heads of the posts, and of ornamental outline of the lower edge of the board. The latest I know in this district bears the date 1861.

2 P

It is much to be regretted that this simple form of monument should have passed out of use. The cast-iron crosses from the ironmonger's pattern-book are but a sorry substitute for the honest piece of carpenter's work, made in the dead man's own village, perhaps by a younger man

GRAVE-BOARDS

of his own blood; in any case by one who was known to him.

It is this invasion of the pattern-book and love of meretricious display that is so regrettably spoiling our churchyards and cemeteries. It was a sad day for the most hallowed spots of English ground, when traders introduced from the Continent, and pushed into public notice those artificial wreaths under half-round glasses that debase and disfigure so many of these sacred places. One cannot blame the poor people who buy them, who have not the

Tomb—Early Nineteenth Century—Thursley

Altar Tombs, 1821—Hascombe

education that would show them that the thing is a vulgarity in itself; and that its flashing glass, repeated all over the churchyard, is a flagrant violation of its precious heritage of beauty and repose. One respects and admires the evident intention of the poor persons who desire in this way (not knowing better) to show affection for their dead; but one still more respects and admires the good taste and firmness of the rector or vicar—whose freehold the churchyard is, and whose duty it is to maintain its dignity and decency—who refuses to allow this kind of unworthy and meretricious ornament to be placed upon its consecrated soil.

After all, these vulgar things represent but a cheap way of honouring the dead; cheap in money and cheaper still in trouble. Once bought and placed they are no trouble to those who place them. It is quite another matter when real flowers are brought and arranged upon a grave by loving hands.

If some of our people could see a French cemetery, with all its horrors of bad taste, vulgarity, and absurdity, they would, I think, cease even to wish to place these things upon graves. For these artificial wreaths have come to us from abroad, and are a part of a series of memorial articles that include even worse—wreaths of beadwork, everlasting flowers arranged in the stiffest and hardest way, and erections like dolls'-houses filled with photographs in frames, and cheap rubbishy articles of every description.

These evils arise from the fact that in a French cemetery —I do not know how it may be in a parish churchyard— the ground is bought by a family 'in perpetuity,' and the owner of the plot may do as he will with it.

In England we have not only the precious tradition of

repose that closely clings about our churchyards, but the safeguard of their being in the absolute guardianship of the clergy. The most passing glance at the places of burial of the two countries would show the most careless observer what a precious thing it is that our own churchyards are so guarded.

I cannot write these words of unfavourable criticism of anything French, without accompanying them by an expression of wonder, that, among a people so distinctly gifted as a nation with a just appreciation of what is beautiful and seemly, and so well trained in their excellent government technical schools, this crying abuse in their treatment of their most sacred places should exist. It is enough to say, as an example, that I have seen as a monument over a grave an iron erection exactly like a hat-stand, with pegs for the holding of bead-work wreaths. Is this honouring the dead?

Let us jealously guard and treasure the quiet beauty and dignity of our country churchyards, and above all keep them from the desecration of anything ill-designed, mean, or tawdry. A rosebush costs less even than an artificial wreath, and is a beautiful and more enduring monument. It may want a little pruning and tending from time to time, but this small trouble will scarcely be grudged 'In loving memory.'

CHAPTER XVIII

THE SMUGGLERS

THOUGH most of the smuggling in this part of England, of which so much went on in the end of the eighteenth and beginning of the nineteenth centuries, passed through the middle of Sussex, some of the goods landed on the western shores of the country came up this way, passing over Highdown Heath and Munstead Heath—wastes of tall gorse, holly, and juniper, stunted oak and thorn and Scotch fir.

These high-lying lands are still scored with the remains of old pack-horse tracks, then well known to the smugglers. A gang would hide in the woody tangles, and one or two of its members would steal out at night to the villages and towns, selling brandy to public-house keepers and private people. They came down to Godalming by Holloway Hill.

In those days there was no police, only a night-watchman, who cried the hours and the state of the weather: 'Past ten o'clock and a starlight night,' and so on.

The smugglers travelled at night, keeping to the woods and heaths and least frequented lanes. Sometimes their path was a scarcely defined track through the heath, sometimes it was worn into a hollow by other and more lawful use, and by the washing of rain. In time, the rain, rushing down steep inclines, cut the track into deep gullies, dangerous for the pack-horses. Then a fresh track

A Woodland Lair

A Thorn Thicket

By Heathy Heights

Through Gorse-Grown Hollows

was taken, on one side of the old one and parallel to it, and so on perhaps three or four times. There are many places about the heaths and woods where evidences of this remain—always on sloping ground.

Some four miles from my home one such set of old

By the Heath Ponds

pack-horse tracks passes near a remarkable smuggler's lair and hiding-place. It lies off the track, well concealed in a wood, in a private property. It is a region of caves, evidently made by human hands, though probably begun by foxes, in the sandy soil just south of the chalk ridge.

IN A SMUGGLER'S LANE

A Woodland Track

Roomy galleries, eight feet high and as much wide, ramble about underground, with ramifications to right and left, and puzzling, deeply-indented bays, and passages that come to a sudden stop. Sometimes a glimmer of light shows at the end of one of these, and is accounted for in the

OLD YEW ON THE CHALK DOWNS

wood above by a deep hollow among the trees, and a hole that might be the entrance of a fox's earth. The labyrinth below has a floor of soft sand, and feels warm and dry in wintry weather. No doubt it had a second practicable exit, and bold, indeed, must have been the excise-men of a hundred years ago who ventured down into its depths when they were held by an armed smuggling gang.

When I was young I used to ride about these beautiful wild places, then all unenclosed. One might ride for half a day without meeting a soul or seeing a house, in natural

THE PILGRIMS' YEWS

untouched forest land, among the thorns and junipers, tangled with wild rose and honeysuckle and garlanded with bryony; past tall dark hollies; or in woodland of mighty beeches. Or northward on the chalk range among the ancient yews; the same trees that five hundred years ago sheltered and guided the pilgrims journeying from the south and west of England to the shrine of St. Thomas of Canterbury.

THE SMUGGLERS

And nearer home again there was the long extent of the Hurtwood and its adjoining wastes—forest land of oak and birch and Scotch fir, with undergrowth of heath and

One of the Pilgrims' Yews

bracken, where the remembrance of the smugglers is still bright in the memories of the working folk.

The windmill on Ewhurst Hill, still standing, was near the middle of the smugglers' tracks. One of the men of the place said his mother remembered a man riding back down the hill above the 'Windmill' Inn, to look for a keg of brandy that had got loose from his pack-load;

also that his father used to tell her how, when a man riding looked very stout, he could make a pretty good guess that he had yards and yards of smuggled silk wound round him.

Another remembered how kegs of brandy were often hid inside an altar-tomb in Cranleigh Churchyard. One night some men concealed themselves in the church porch to watch for and catch the smugglers, but when the smugglers came, their courage evaporated, and not a man dared stir.

Many squires and yeomen were friendly with the smugglers, and it was known that kegs of brandy were often left on the doorstep at Barhatch in the time of the last of the Ticknor family, whose ancestors built the house in the reign of Queen Elizabeth. Here there is also a dog-gate at the stair-foot; another, a few miles away, is shown at p. 34.

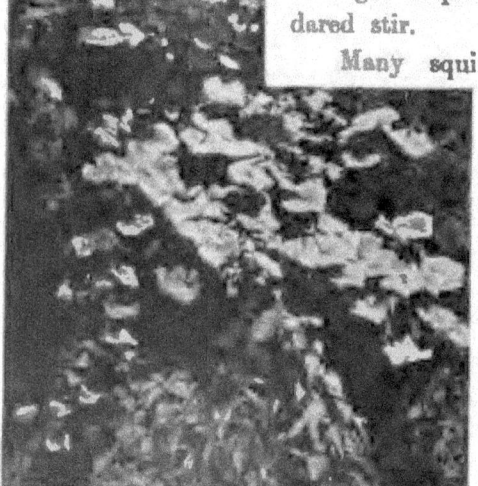

BLACK BRYONY

An old shepherd who worked on the chalk downs a few miles to the north, who was eighty-two years of age in 1889, told how smugglers used to bring their pack-loads of brandy up Combe Bottom and hide them among the thickets of juniper, thorn, and bramble.

THE SMUGGLERS

They came up from Shoreham Water, riding into the sea at high tide and loading the horses straight from the boats.

They passed just behind this shoulder of the Downs, and would ride up into the Hurtwood the same night—right across Sussex and a few miles over. As the crow flies it is twenty-five miles, and who knows how much more by the devious ways they had to follow. They got

A SHOULDER OF THE DOWNS

up to the wooded heights either by Jelley's Hollow or Horseblock Hollow, or up by the 'Windmill' Inn.

This inn, originally a lonely cottage, was a favourite resort of theirs. It was first known as the 'New Inn.' To this day it has the false roof for hiding smuggled goods.

A hundred years ago it was a very rough and lawless set of people that lived in the hamlet of Peaslake, that lies in a northern hollow of the Hurtwood, and in the scattered cottages in the neighbouring forest land—a tract from six to seven miles long. They were descendants of wandering gipsy people; all smugglers and poachers, and the terror of the quiet farm people about Ewhurst.

An old woman, who died in 1888 at the age of eighty-two, related how, when she was a girl, when smoke was

OLD TRACK, NOW A GOOD ROAD

seen rising from a certain empty cottage on the heath-covered slopes above, they all knew that 'the Peaslake men were having a night of it;' feasting on a stolen pig or poultry, and they 'lay trembling in their beds.' These rough people seem to have been the natural enemies of the agricultural folk below.

As late as the year 1891 there was an old man living in a neighbouring village who in his youth had been transported for smuggling. Another man at about the same time, also transported, left his locked box at his master's, who had it nailed down to the floor with hoop-iron. It was never claimed.

Now that the district has become so much more populous, there are good roads where formerly there was only the roughest lane or forest track. The one in the picture has only become a well-kept road within my recollection.

When the country people discovered the hiding-place of contraband goods, the result of a successful 'run,' it was customary for the finder to put a chalk mark on a small proportion of the number of articles. When the smugglers went again to collect their kegs, the marked ones were left. This was well understood as a bargain, in consideration of the discovery not being reported.

A squire, new to the country, came to live at a place in the hills near Dorking in the early part of the nineteenth century. One morning, before he was dressed, his valet brought him an urgent message from the bailiff to say that he wished to see him. The master said he must wait, as he was not dressed. The message came again, still more pressingly worded.

'Well, send the fellow up,' said the unfinished squire.

The man came in with a mysterious air and watched the servant out of the room, and then said in a hoarse half-whisper: '*There was a run last night, sir, and I've marked four.*'

The squire had not the least idea what the information meant, and on being enlightened he burst out indignantly: 'But I can't have anything to do with smuggled goods; why, I'm a magistrate. How dare you come to me with such a suggestion.'

The bailiff stood his ground quite unabashed. 'If you'll take my word for it, sir, if you don't do as others do, you'll have trouble.'

The squire continuing to protest vigorously, the bailiff said, 'Well, sir, will you ask the parson?'

He did so, and the rector's answer was: '*If you wish to live in peace with your neighbours you had better fall in with the custom of the country.*'

INDEX

ALTAR-TOMBS, 287
Autobiography, a cottager's, 233

BABY-RUNNER, 67
Bacon, smoking, 16; bacon-loft, 16, 19
Bargain, 243
Bargate, slabs, 11, 21; stone, 39
Barn, 22; barn-shovel, 22; floor, 23
Bedsteads, 64
Bed-waggon, 72
Bee-hive, 163; makers, 164
Beer-jug, 144
Bellows, 97, 98, 99
Bell-ringer, 243
Bird-cage, 74
Bird names, local, 221
Blind needlewoman, 230
Bludgeon, 179
Blunderbuss, 293
Bonnet, sun, 249, 255; Sunday, 250
Bottles, stoneware, 145; wooden, 189; leather, 193; glass, 291
Bowbrick, 8
Boxes, brass, 136; work, 137; tea, 137; painted, 139; money, 139, 140; domino, 140
Boys scaring birds, 237; boys' clothing, 257
Brand-tongs, 95
Breweries, 295
Bricklayers, 201
Bricks, old and new, 5
Bristol ware, 147
Brooms, birch and heath, 166
Buckles, shoe, 249
Bullock-teams, 216
Butcher, 242
Butter-scales, wooden, 164; butter-prints, 165; butter-scoop, 165

CANDLE-BOX, 109
Candles, 109

Candlesticks, brass, 109, 112; hanging, 110; kitchen, 112; jointed, 112; plated, 177
Cap, 249, 252
Carriers, 294
Carters, 211
Carter's frock, 258
Carter's horse-talk, 216
Cat, 70
Cauldron, cheese, 83, 92
Caves, smugglers', 306
Chair, Windsor, 56, 57, 58; rush-bottomed, 59, 60, 61; angle, 62; oak and mahogany, 169, 172; bamboo-pattern, 172
Cheerfulness, 244, 277
Cheese room, 20
Chest of drawers, 54
Children, their labour, 237; discipline, 237; manners, 237; games, 238; dress, 257
Chimney ornaments, 117, 119
Chimneys, 5; chimney-bar, 79, 82; crane, 79, 81, 82
China, old pieces, 173
Church bells, 228
Churchyards, 296 and onward
Cider, 21, 189; cider-mill, 196; cider-press, 196
Clocks, 62; Dutch, 65
Clothes-hutch, 54
Clothing, 249 and onward
Coaches, 288, 293
Cobbett, William, 237
Cocoa-nuts, carved, 291
Coffee-mill, 68
Cooking implements, 73
Copse-cutting, 196
Cottages, 1 and onward; of one room, 7, 8; timber-framed, 1, 30, 40; old and new, 43; cottage fireside, 79; gardens, 268

INDEX

Country folk, 218; speech, 219 and onward
Cow-jug, 118
Cradle, oak, 67
Crockery, 141 and onward
Cup-dogs, 83

DAIRY, 20
'Dame Wiggins,' 64, 68, 76, 95
Demijohn, 292
Desk, oak, 54; standing, 55
Dibbling-iron, 185; dibbling wheat, 185
Dog-gate, 33
Dog spears, 280
Door-scrapers, 11
Dorsetshire Pills, 147
'Down' fireplace, 19
Dredgers, brass, 136
Dresser, 53
Driving past long loads, 205
Drop-handle, 33, 65
Drying-line, 162

EARTHENWARE, red, 146; pitchers, 146; Dorsetshire, 147; washing-pan, 160

FAG-HOOK, 156, 183
Fairs, 119, 244; Godalming fair-day, 243; 'Heffel' fair-day, 245
Farmhouse, 15 and onward; kitchen, 19
Fashion, 263
Fat for rushlights, 11
Fence, post and rail, 25
Fights, 244
Fire-backs, 86
Fire-dogs, 83
Fire-irons, 95
Fish-vans, 293; dog-drawn fish-carts, 294
Flail, 23, 185
Flint and steel, 107
Flint-lock for striking light, 115
Food, 46, 237, 239, 241
French cemeteries, 301
French names, 88, 257
Frying-pan, 93
Furniture, 44 and onward

GARNETED JOINTS, 39
Gate, five-barred, 28
Gipsies, 264
Girls, at service, 240; dress, 257, 258
Glasses, 174
Gleaning, 187
Godalming, 282 and onward
Granary, 34, 187
Grave-boards, 297
Grease-pans, 101

HANDKERCHIEF, 254, 265
Hangers, 82
'Happy England,' Mrs. Allingham's, 8, 258
Harvest-bottles, 189
Hay-rakes, 156, 181
Hazel sticks, bills notched on, 225
Hearth, 'down,' 19; iron hearthplate, 19
Heath-cutter, 201
Hog-form, 57, 242
Home industries, 157
Hoop-making, 196
Horns, drinking, 192
Horse ornaments, 211; ear-caps, 214; harness, 214; shoes, 215
Horsham slabs, 4, 16
Hour-glass, 174
Hurdle-making, 198
Hutch, linen, 48; clothes, 54

IDLE-BACK, 99
Ink-pots, 137
Inn, village, 245; in Godalming, 248
Iron, smoothing, 74; stand, 74
Iron box, 179
Iron-room, 21
Iron-stone, 11, 12

JOINT-STOOL, 48
Jugs, Toby, 117; Bristol, 147; 'Dipped' ware, 148; lustre, 154; farm, 155

KETTLE-HOLDER, 131
Kettle-tipper, 99
Kitchen, farm, 19, 79
Kitchen, table, 20, 45
Knife-box, 68
Knife-tray, 68

INDEX

LABOURERS' WAGES, 238, 239; food, 239; long hours, 240; clothing, 262, 264
Landscape pattern ware, 151
Lanterns, 78
Latten bells, 213
Leaden ventilator, 20
Leg-irons, 179
Lime for land, 208
Lime-kilns, 208
Linen-hutch, 48
Looking-glass, 116
Lustre ware, 153

MANNER, old country, 218, 243
Man-trap, 281
Master, a good, 241
Matches, sulphur, 107; Congreve, 109
Measures, variety of, 184
Mill, 35
Mole-trap, 209
Mortars, 176
Mouse-traps, 71
Mowers, 189; their meals, 189
Mowing, price of, 189
Mugs, stoneware, 144; earthenware, 150; horn, 192

NAMES, Bible, 257
Needlework, 230; patchwork, 126; samplers, 119; kettle-holder, 131; application, 131
Nut-crackers, 73

OAK, bark for tanning, 16; tile-pins, 168
Oven, brick, 19, 76; peel, 78

PATCHWORK, 126 and onward, 230
Pattens, 256
Paving, 11, 12, 21
Pepper-pots, brass, 136; pewter, 137
Pewter, 174
Pictures, 132
Pins in witchcraft, 229
Pipe, 79
Pipe-rack, 74
Plough, wooden, 185
Posting, 288
Pot, iron, 83
Potato-raker, 95

Prayer-book, 252
Public-house, 245, 246

QUILTS, patchwork, 126

RATTLE, 179
Reaping, 183
Reaping-hook, 156, 182
Reaping tools, old and new, 181
Rick-settle, 24
Rickyard, 24
Road, foundation, 295
Road-waggons, 294
Roofing-tiles, 4, 5
Rough music, 230
'Rozzling,' 199
Rushes, 101
Rushlights, 101
Rushlight-holders, 102; standing, 105; wooden, 107
Rush-work, 168

SACK-LIFTER'S feat, 239
Sailors, 290
Salt-box, 68
Salt-cellars, 137
Samplers, 120 and onward
Saw-pit, 194
Scissors, 73
Scutcheons, handle and keyhole, 65
Scythe, 181, 188
Seed-lip, 22
Settles, 245
Sheep-bell, 187, 200
Sheep-marking iron, 200
Shepherd's crook, 199
Shoddy clothing, 260
Sickle, 156, 182
Signs, 246
Skewers, 73
Skillets, 89
Smith's apron, 262
Smock-frock, 258
Smoothing irons, 160
Smugglers, 303 and onward
Snuffers, 73, 113
Song, ploughman's, 247
Special constable's staff, 177
Speech, old country, 219 and onward
Spigot, 165
Spinning-wheel, 157

Spit, 84; spit-rack, 84
Spode's ware, 151
Spoons, brass, 137; wooden, 165
Spring guns, 279
Staffordshire white ware, 155
Steelyard, 200
Stile, 29
Stocks at Shalford, 180
Stockton 'dipped' ware, 148
Stone, Bargate, 39; slabs, 11, 21; paving, 11, 12; iron, 11, 12; ripple-marked, 12
Stone bottles, 144
Stoneware, mugs, 141; Nottingham, 144; pipkins, 146
Straw-crusher, 160
Straw-plaiting, 160
Style, local, 5
Sugar-nippers, 73
Sunbonnet, 249
Sunday clothes, 260
Sunderland ware, 147
Swarm of bees, 164

TABLE, kitchen, 20, 45; eight-legged, 47; round oak, 47; children's, 48; three-legged, 53
Teaspoons, brass, 137
Thatch, 8, 206;
Threshing, 22; with flail, 185
Tile-hanging, 4, 34
Tile-pins, 168
Timber-waggon, 202; loading, 204
Tinder, 108
Tinder-box, 107; brass tinder-box, 109

Toasting-forks, 93; implement, 93, 95
Tobacco-box, 245
Toby jug, 117
Tolling, 228
Tradition, 5
Traps, 278, 281
Trays, lacquer and mahogany, 173; papier-maché, 173
Trenchers, 46, 237
Trivets, 93

UNSTEAD FARM, 15

WAGES, labourers', 238; farm men, 239; mechanics', 238
Warming-pan, 72
Watchman, 303
Water-mill, 35
Weather-tiling, 4, 34
Weddings, 264
Wedgwood's willow and landscape ware, 151; black ware, 154
Wells, 15, 20
Wheat, 24; dibbled, 185
Willow pattern ware, 151
Winder, flax, 157; for silk, 159
Windmill, Ewhurst, 311
Window plants, 271
Windsor chair, 56
Winnowing-fan, 231
Witchcraft, 229
Wool manufacture, 294
Wyatt's Almshouses, 34

YEWS, the Pilgrims', 310

THE END

www.ingramcontent.com/pod-product-compliance
Lightning Source LLC
Chambersburg PA
CBHW021142160426
43194CB00007B/658